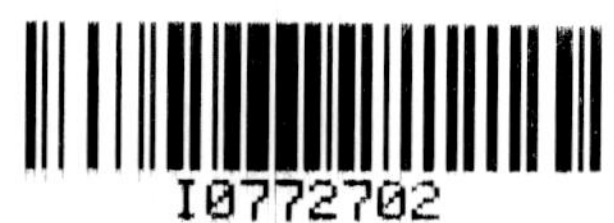

Coloring book for adults and kid s
35 amazing lotus flowers

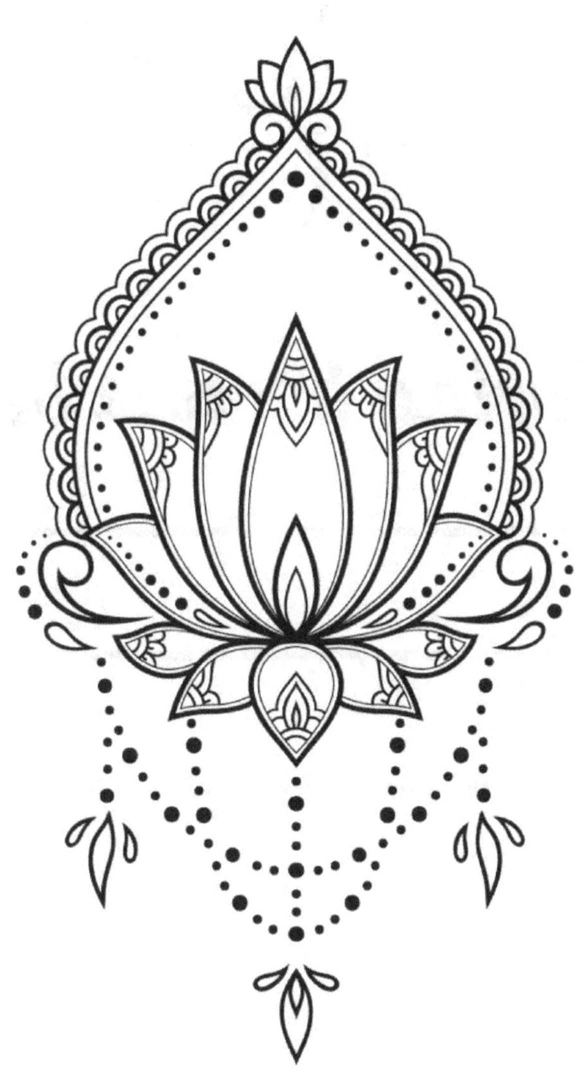

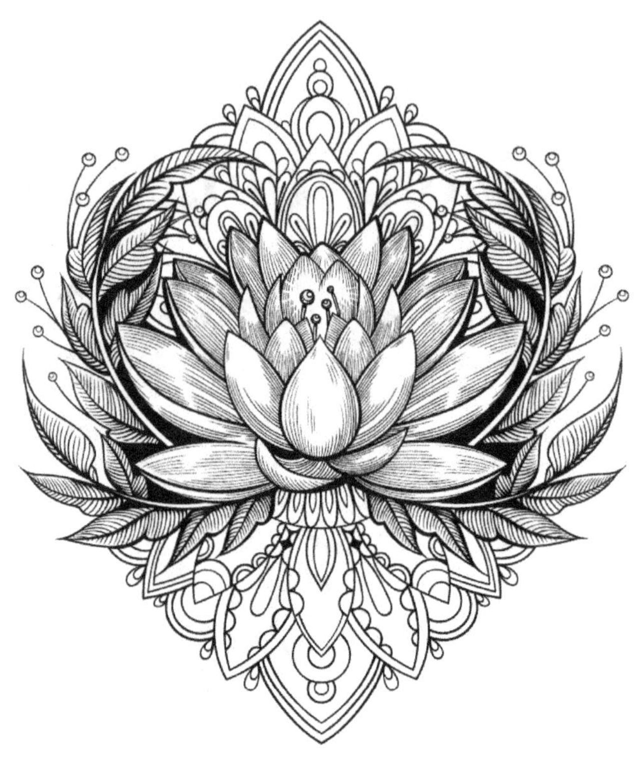

This coloring book is belongs to

____

____

____

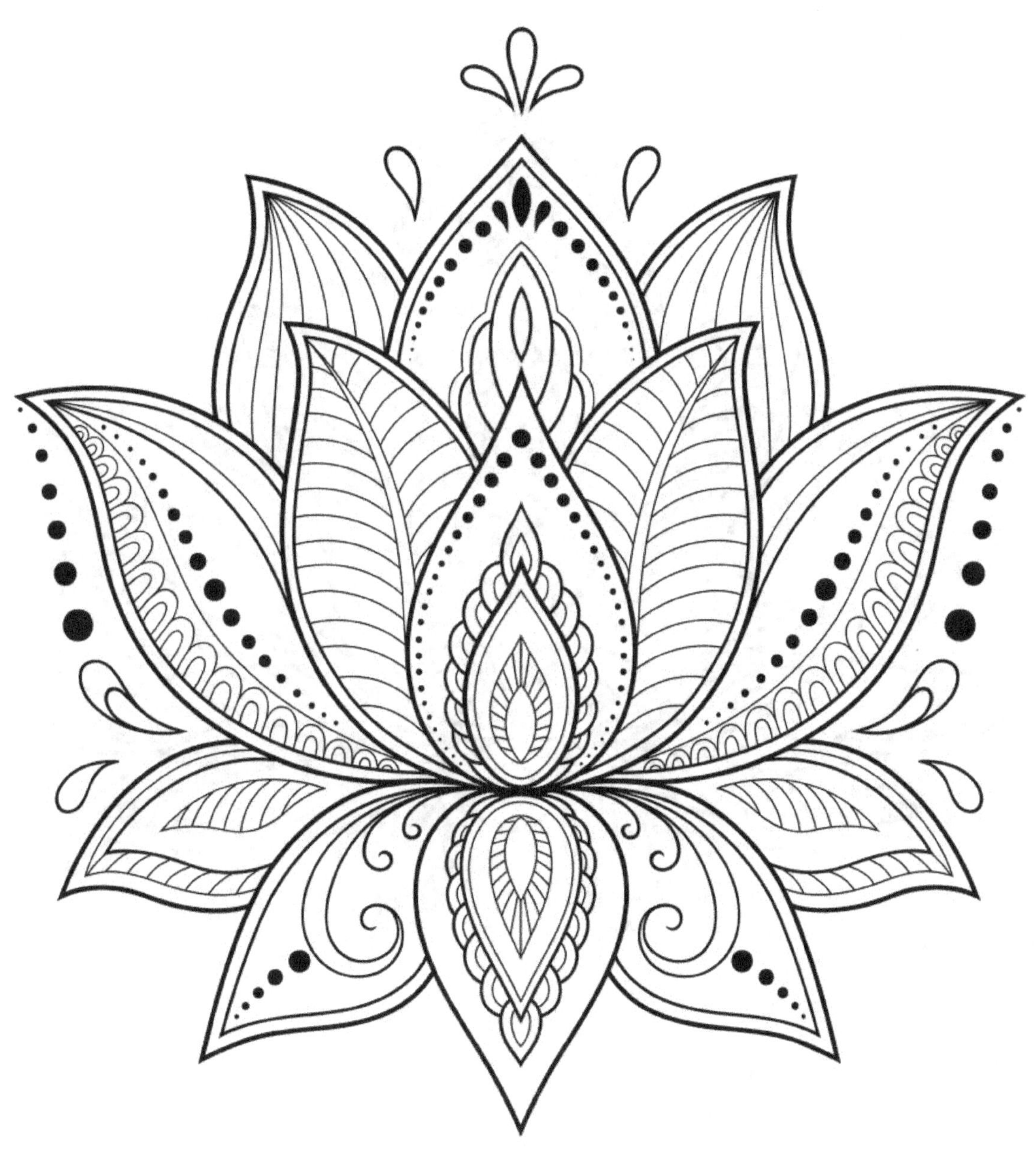

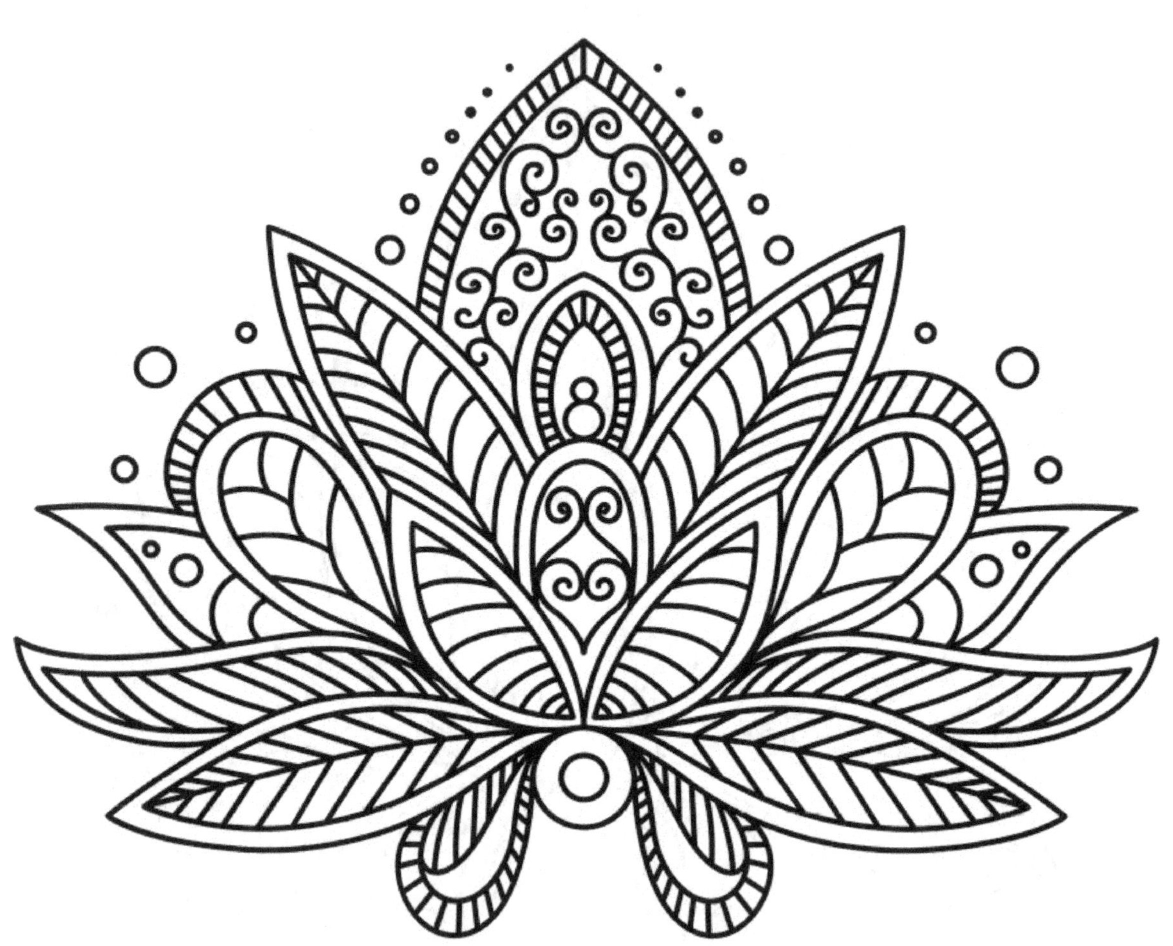

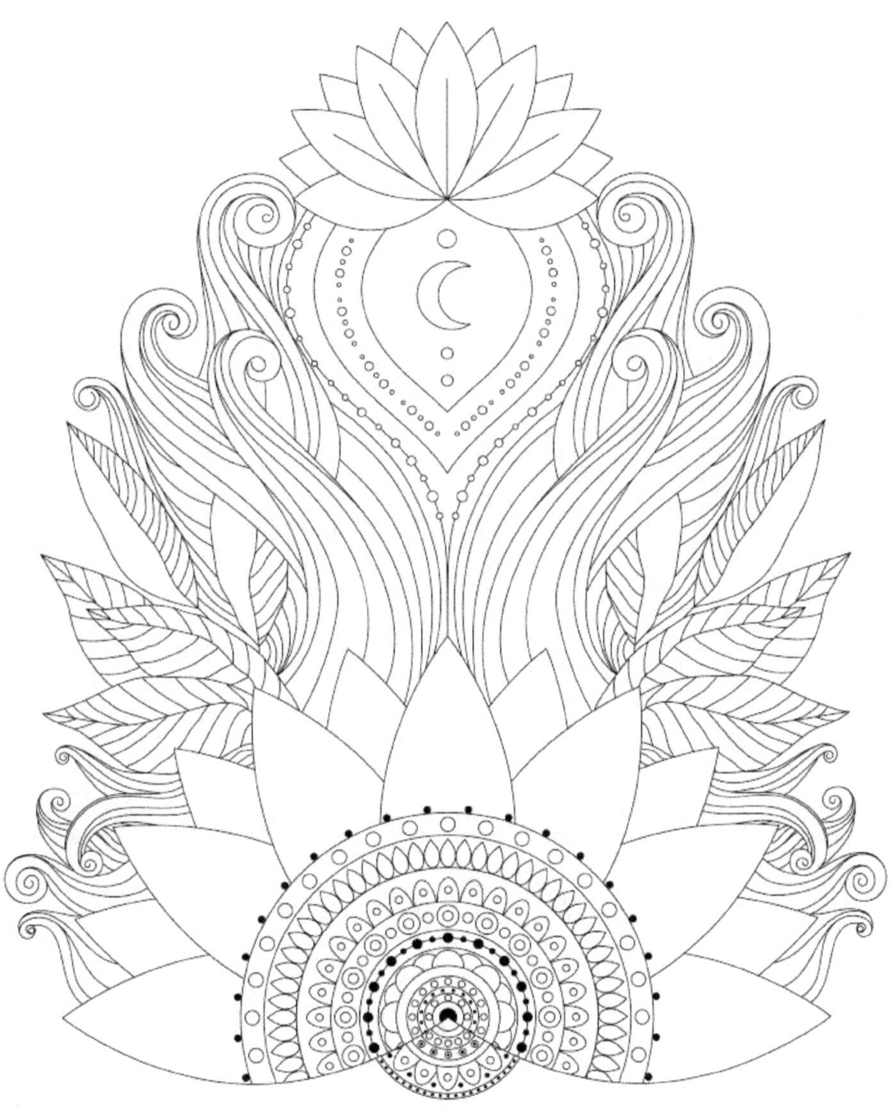

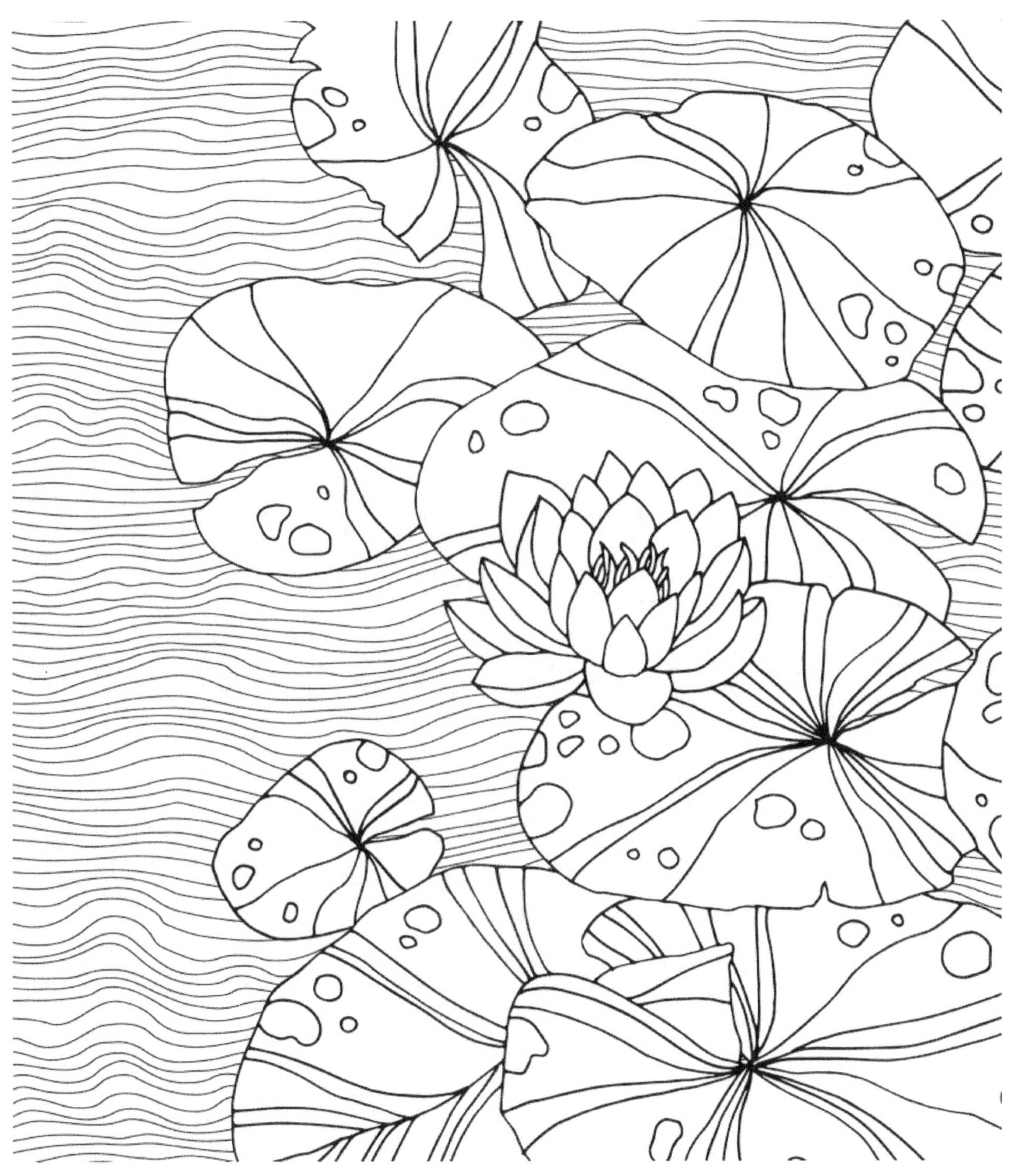

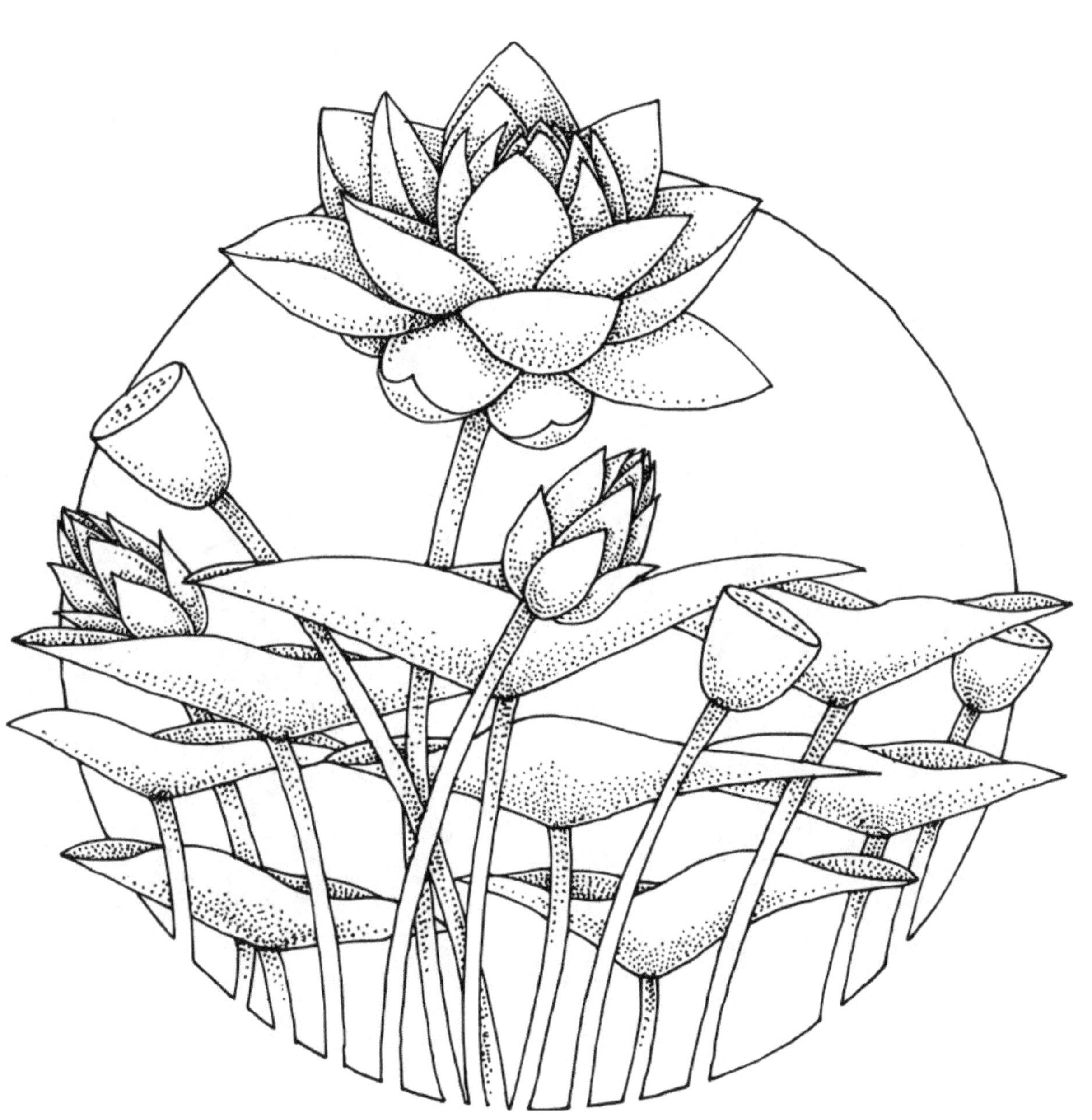

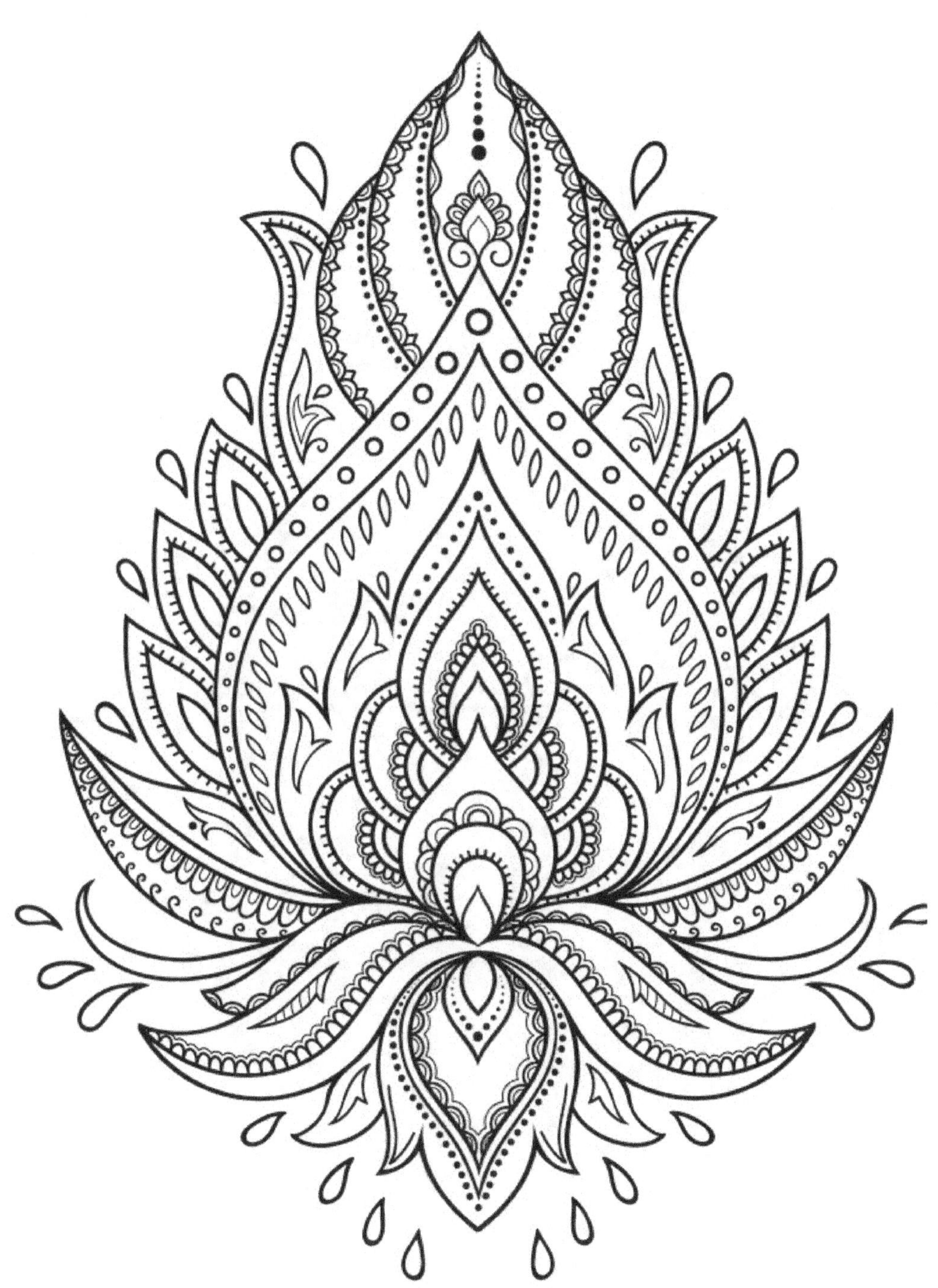

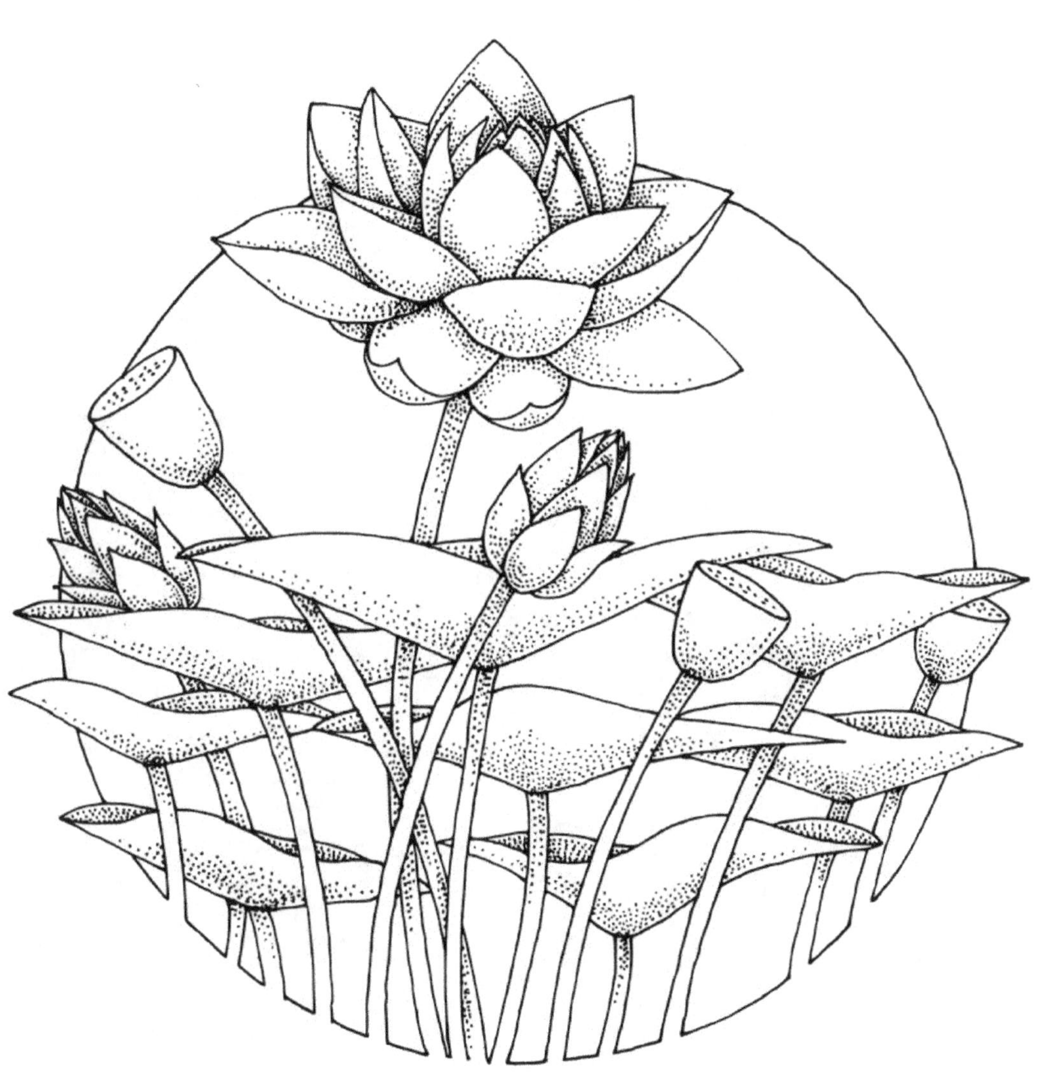

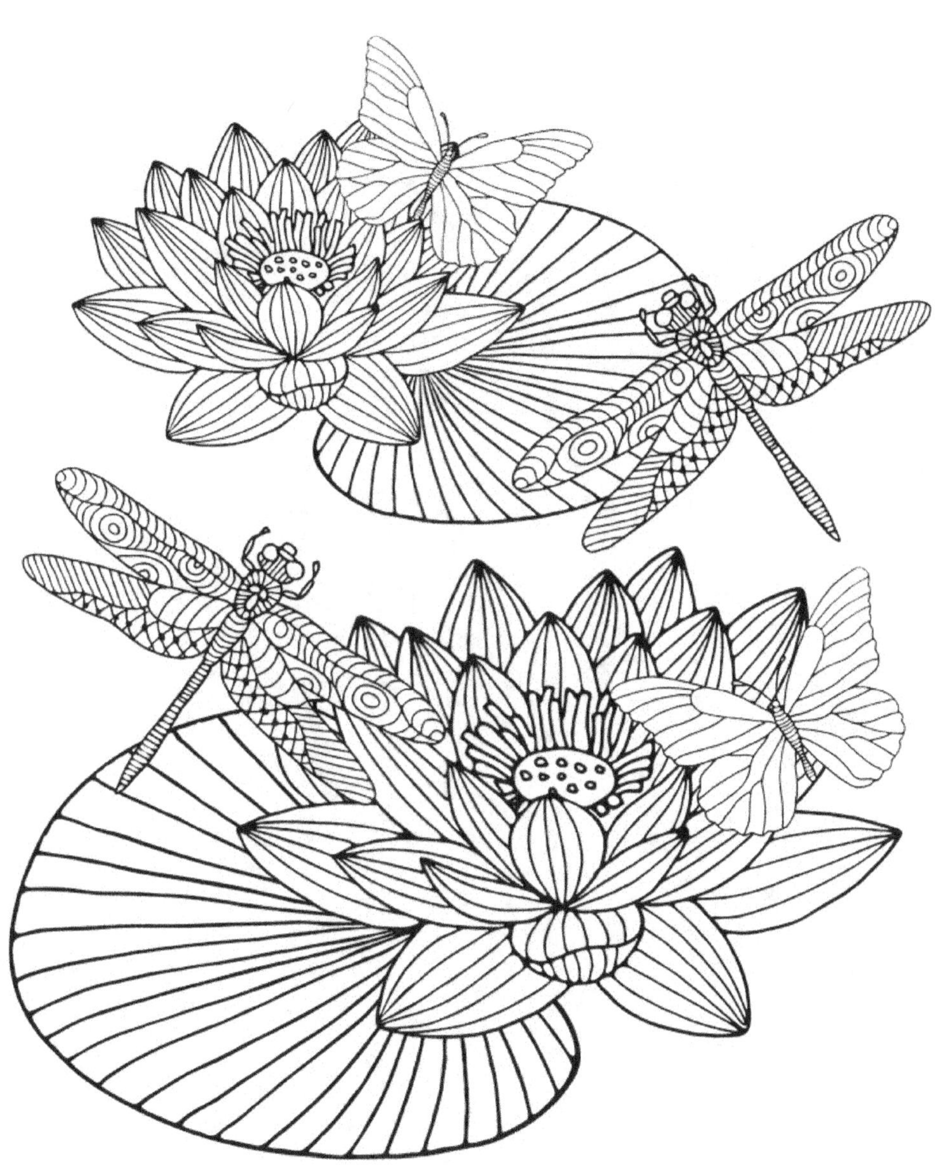

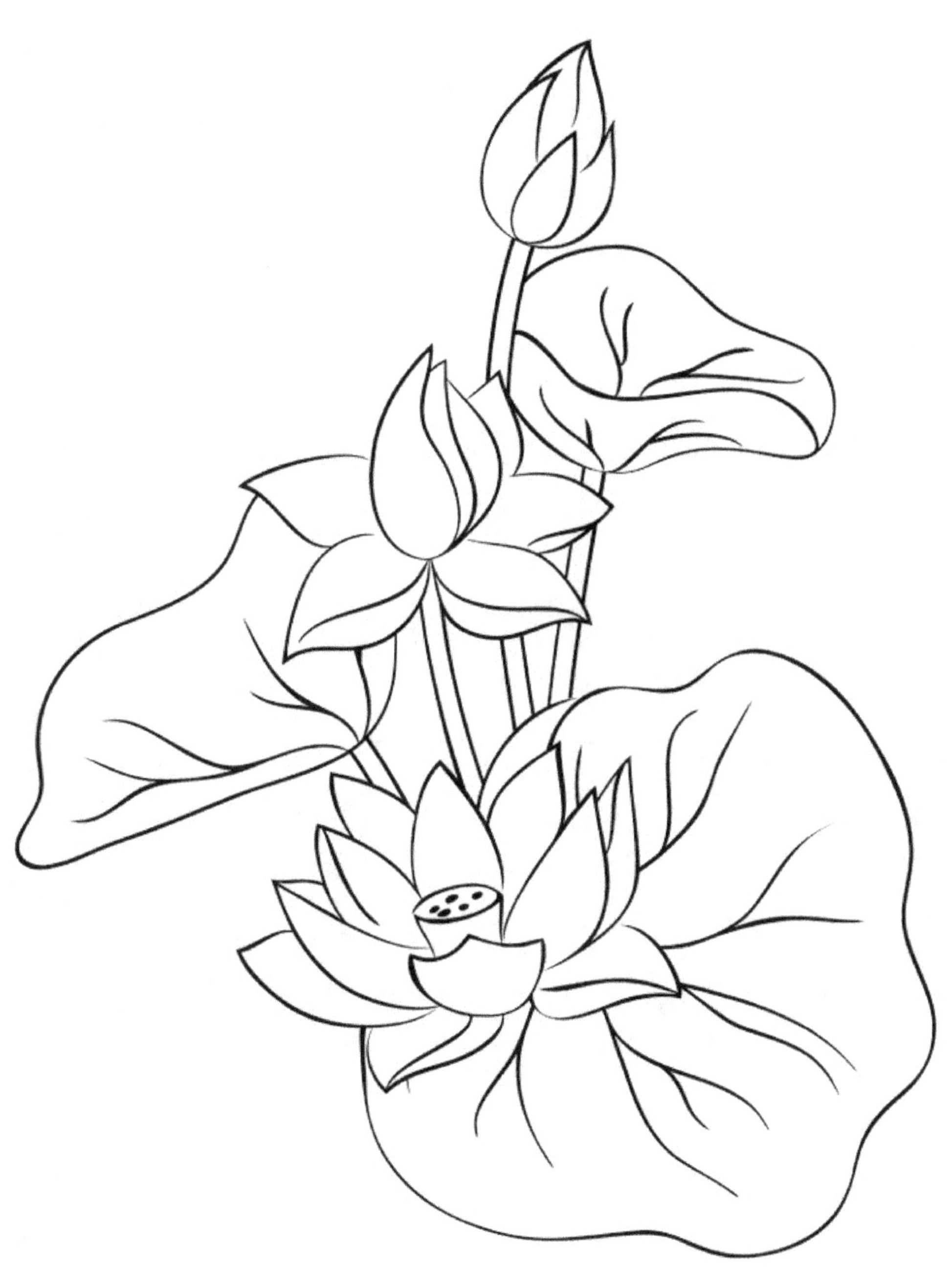

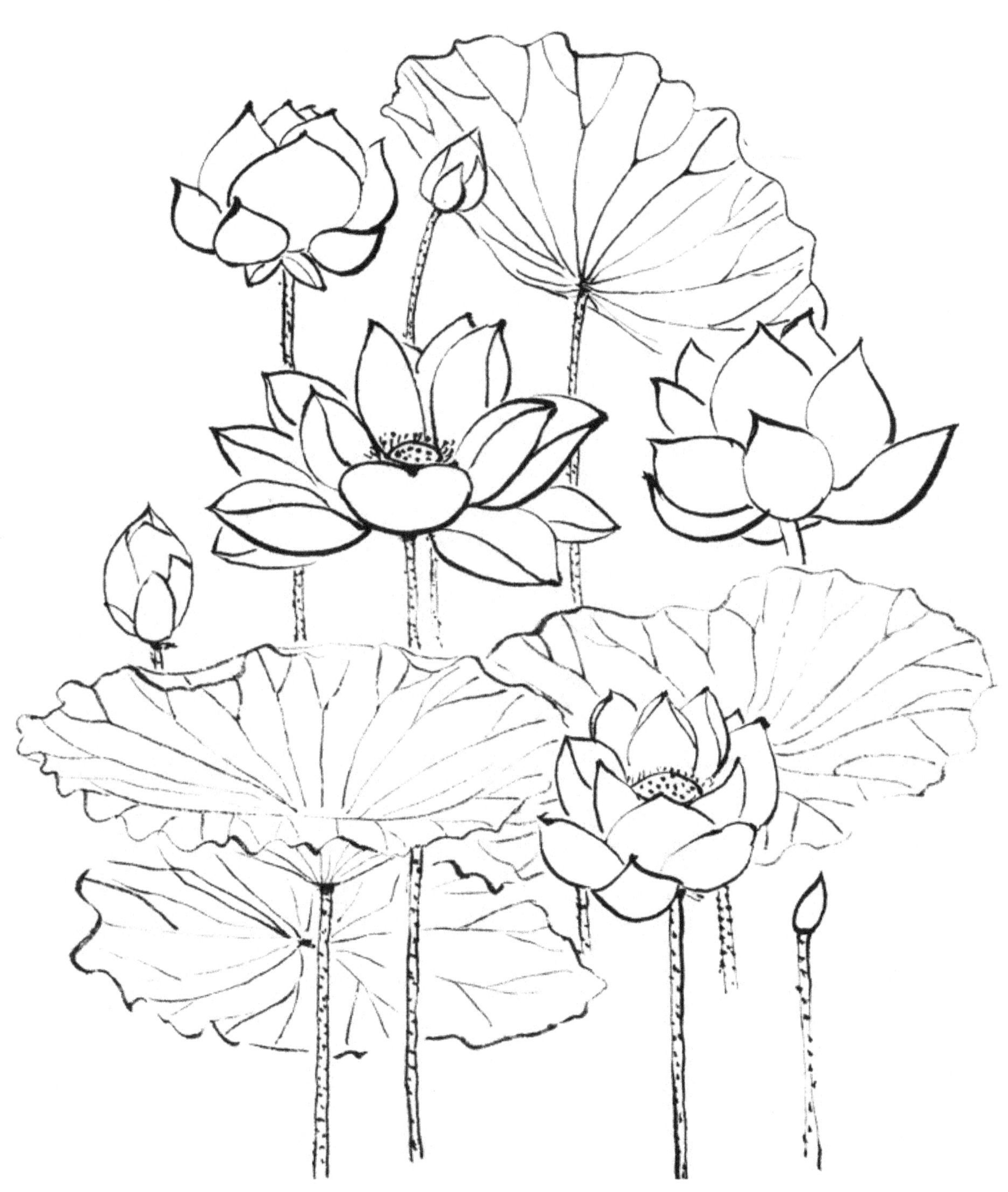

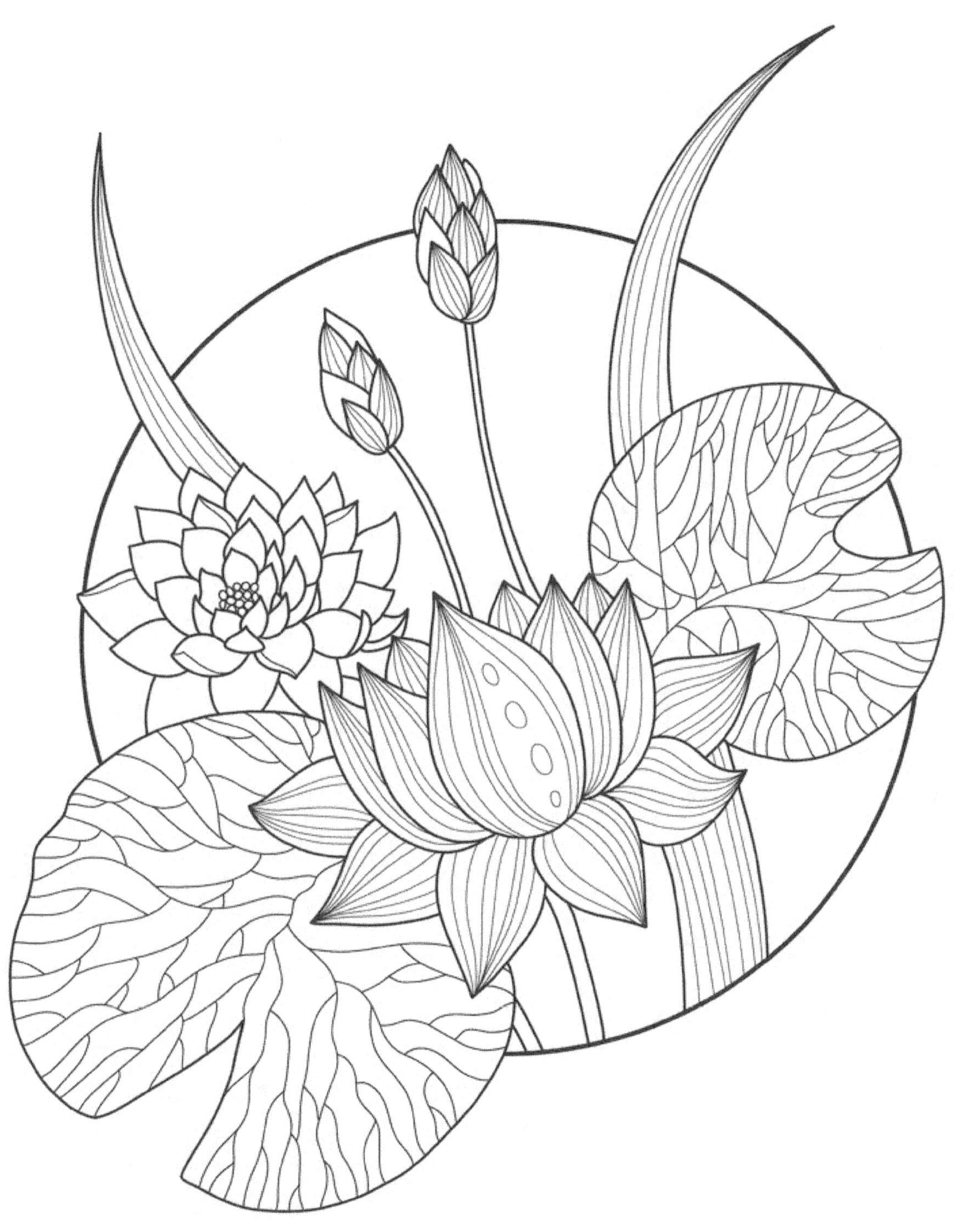

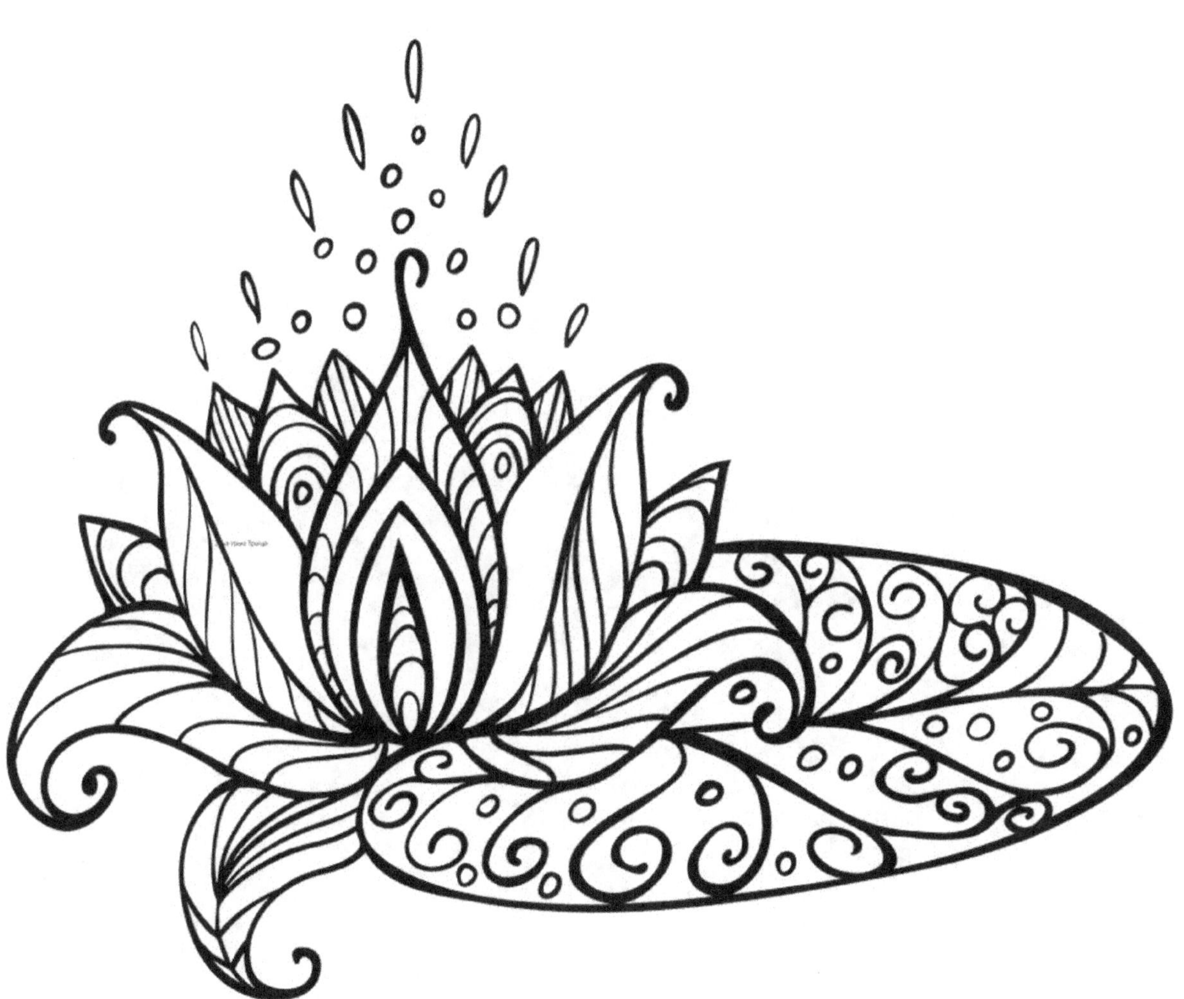

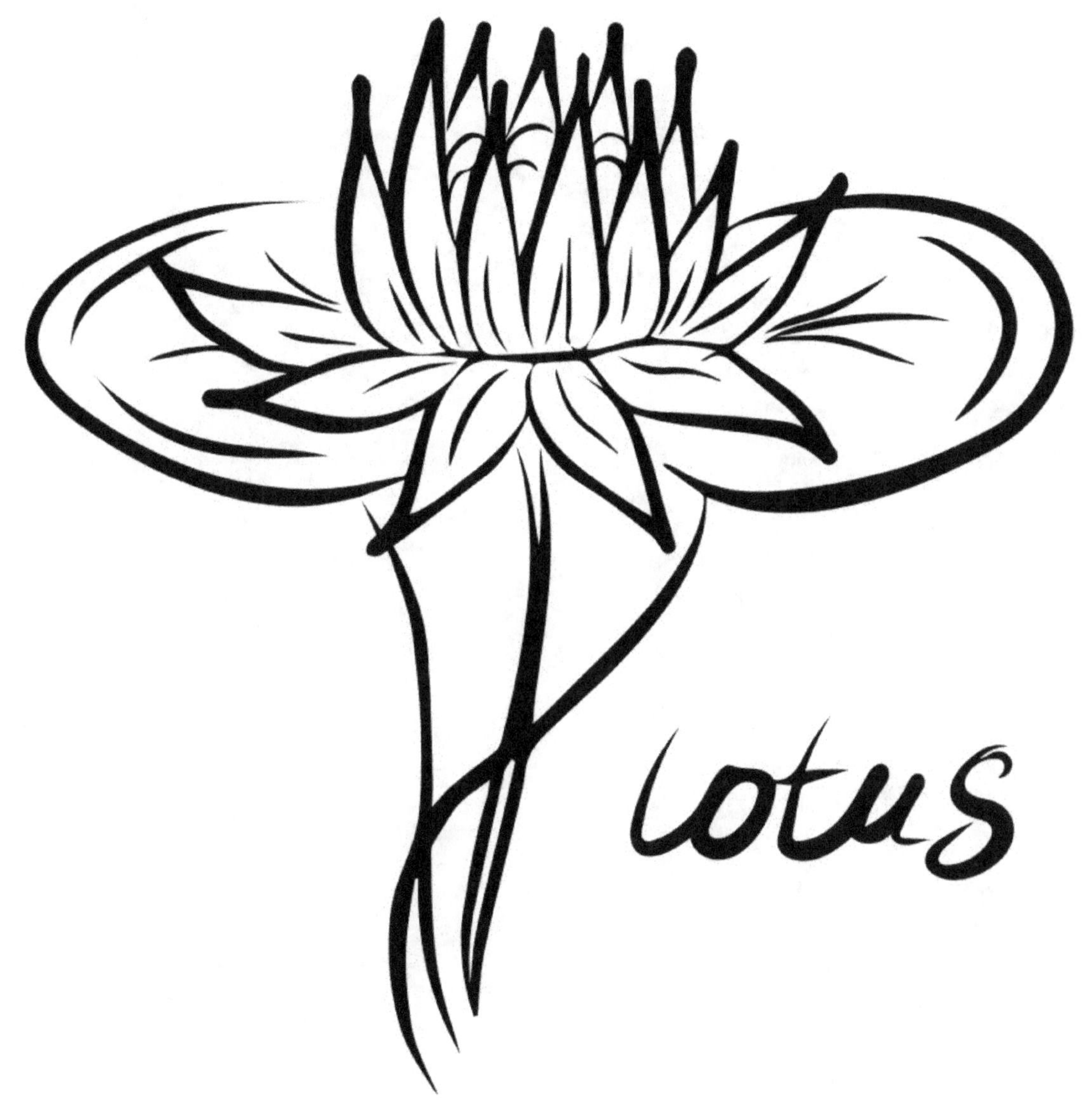

lotus

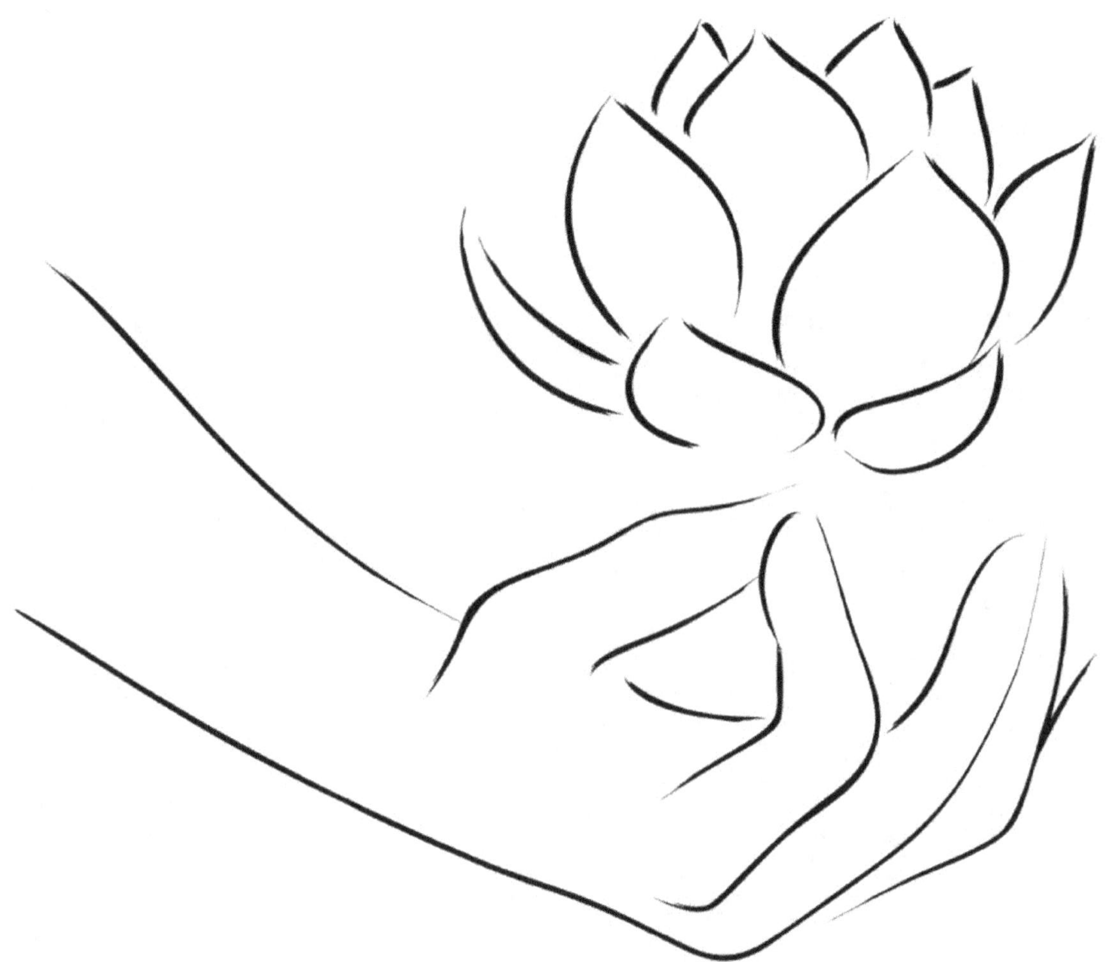

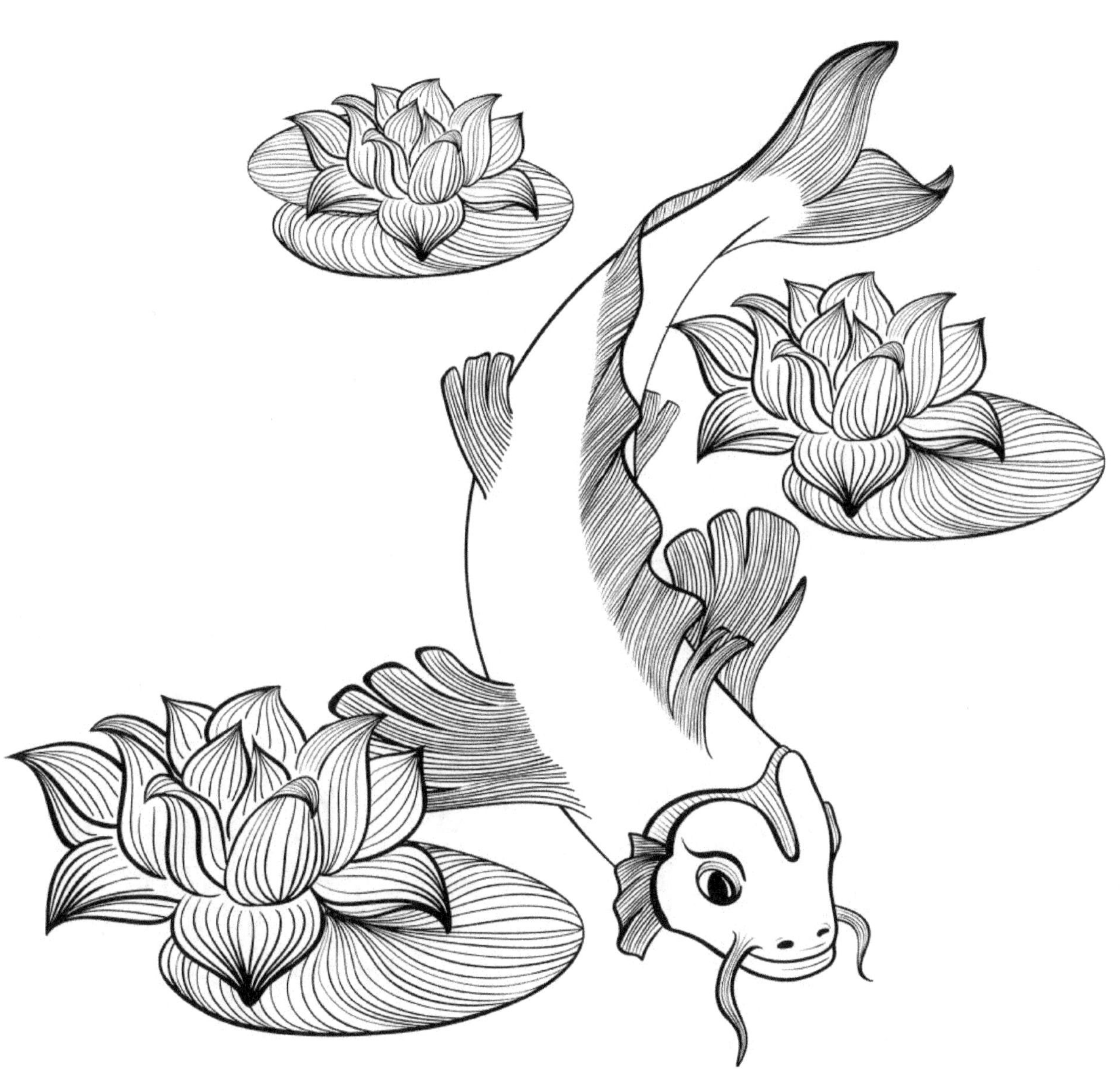

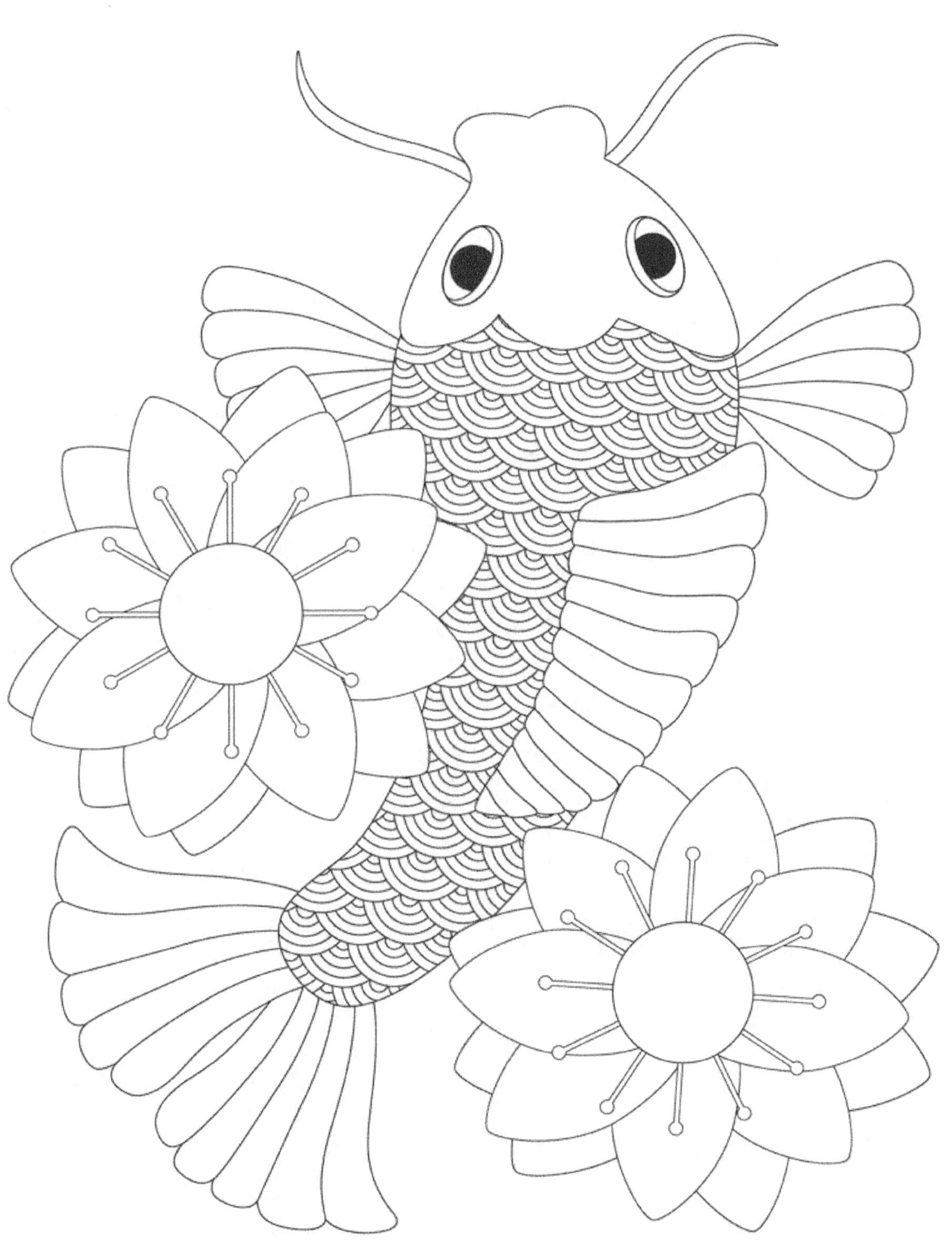

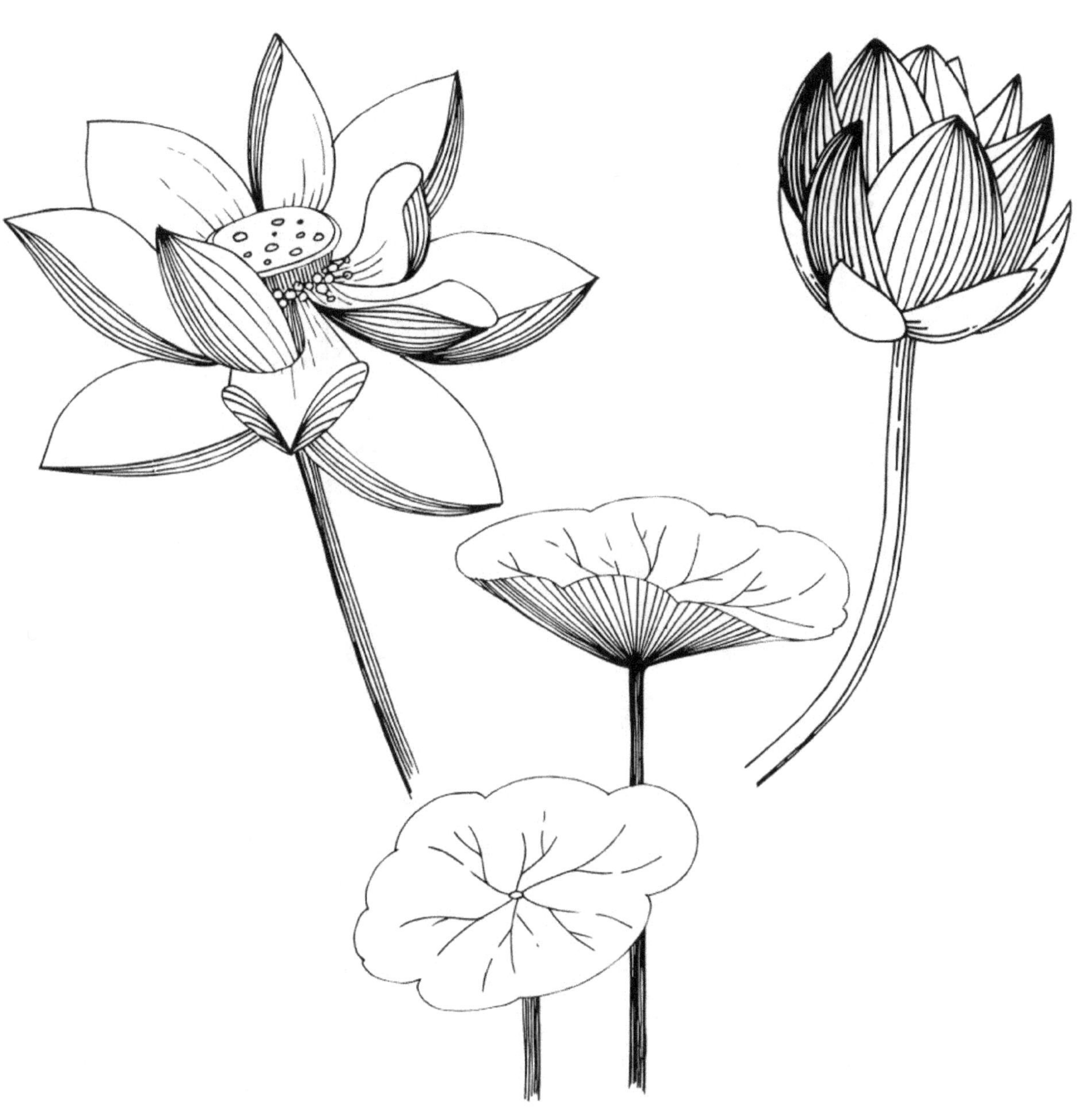

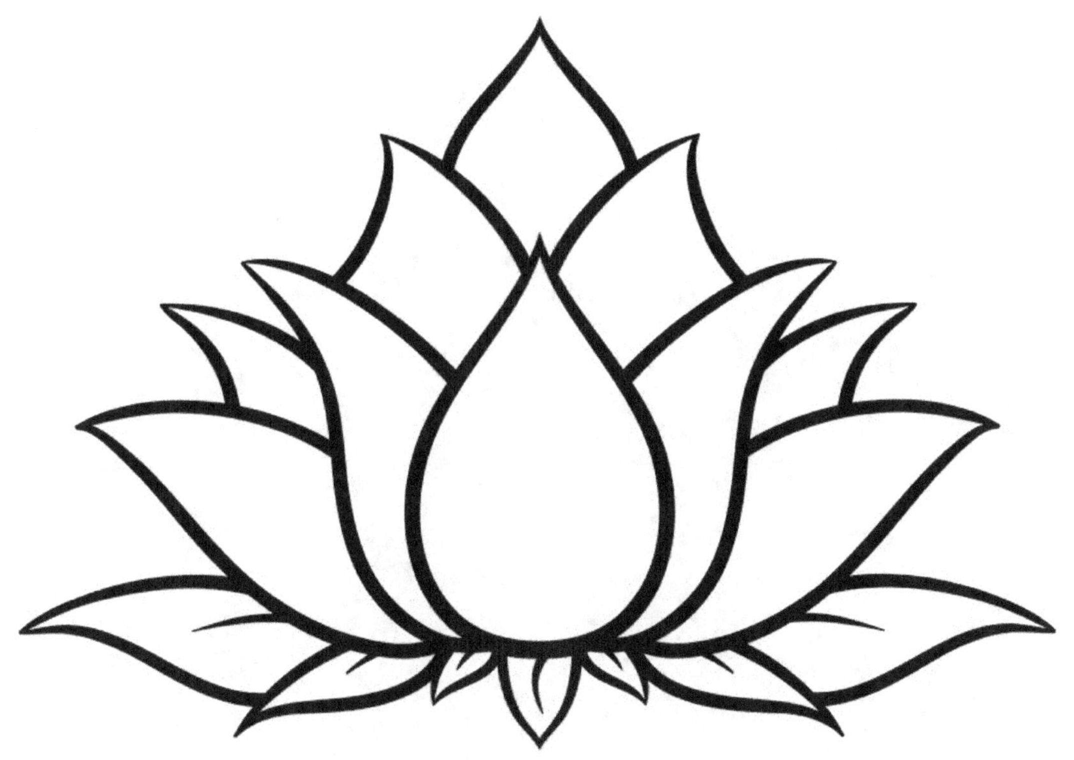

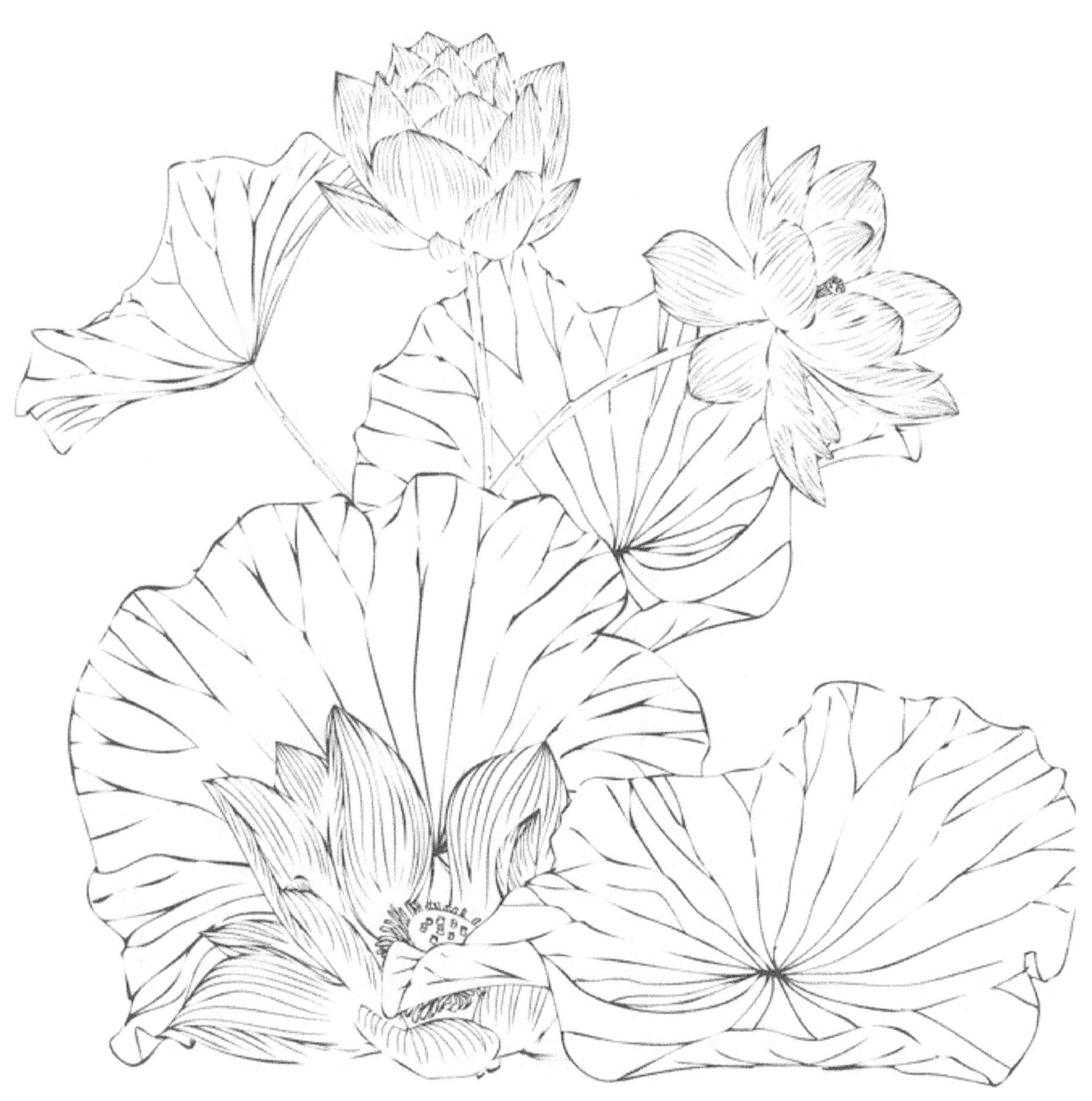

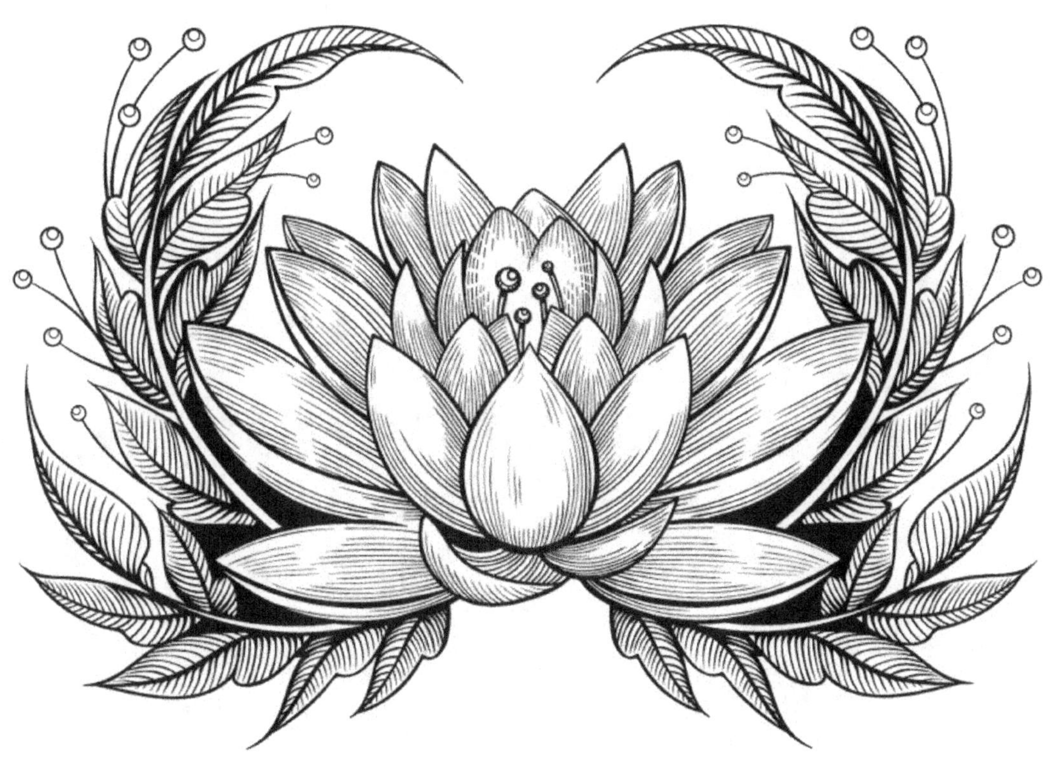

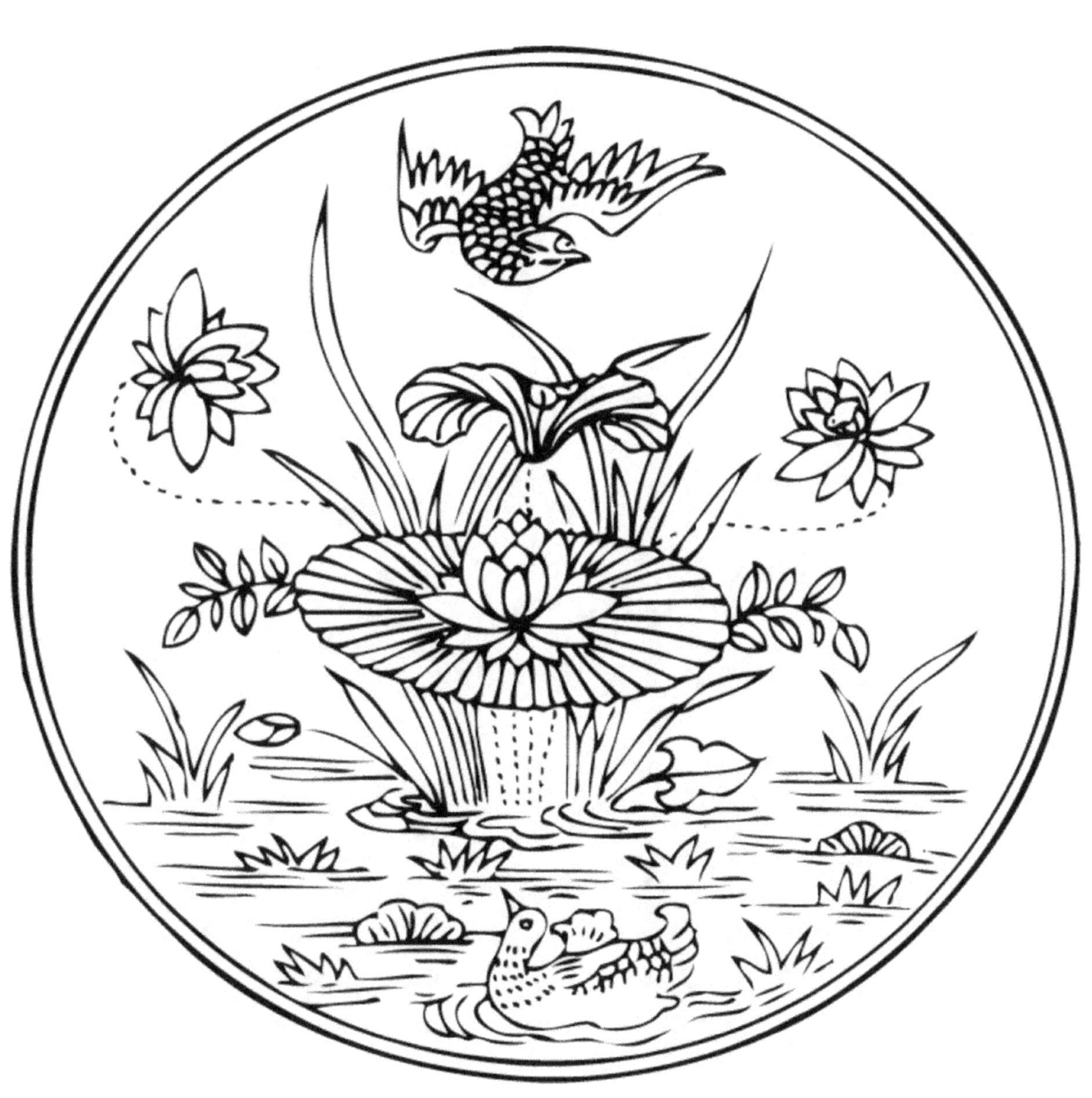

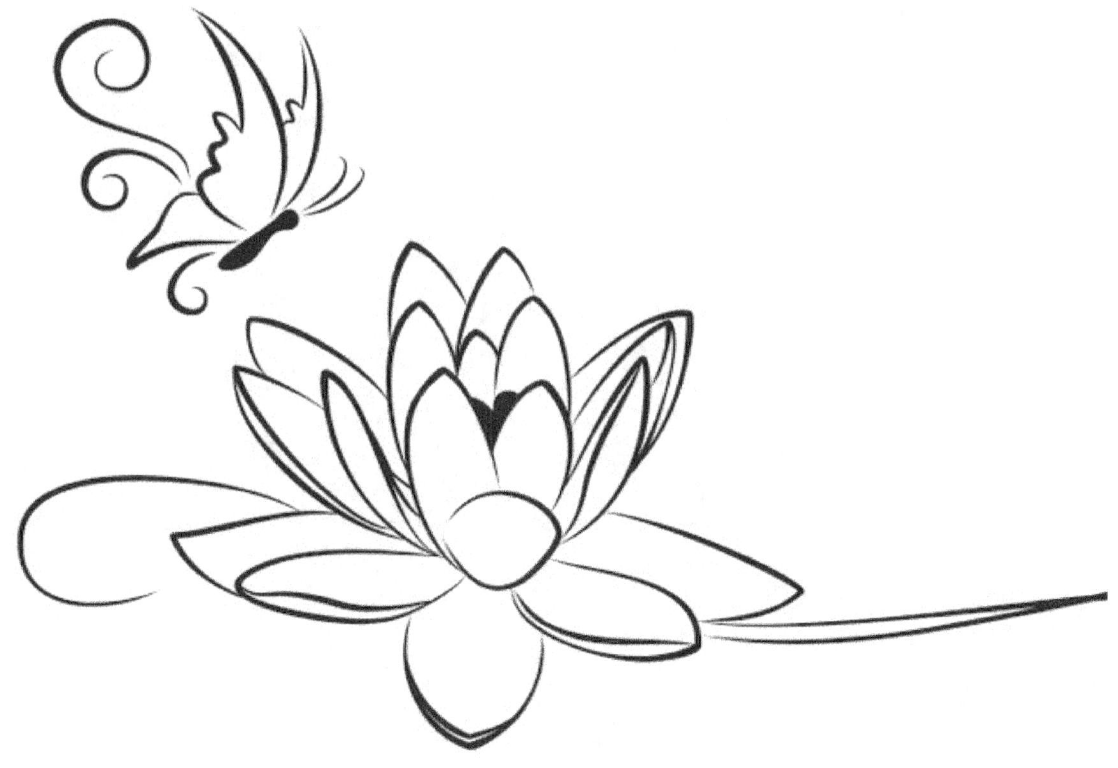

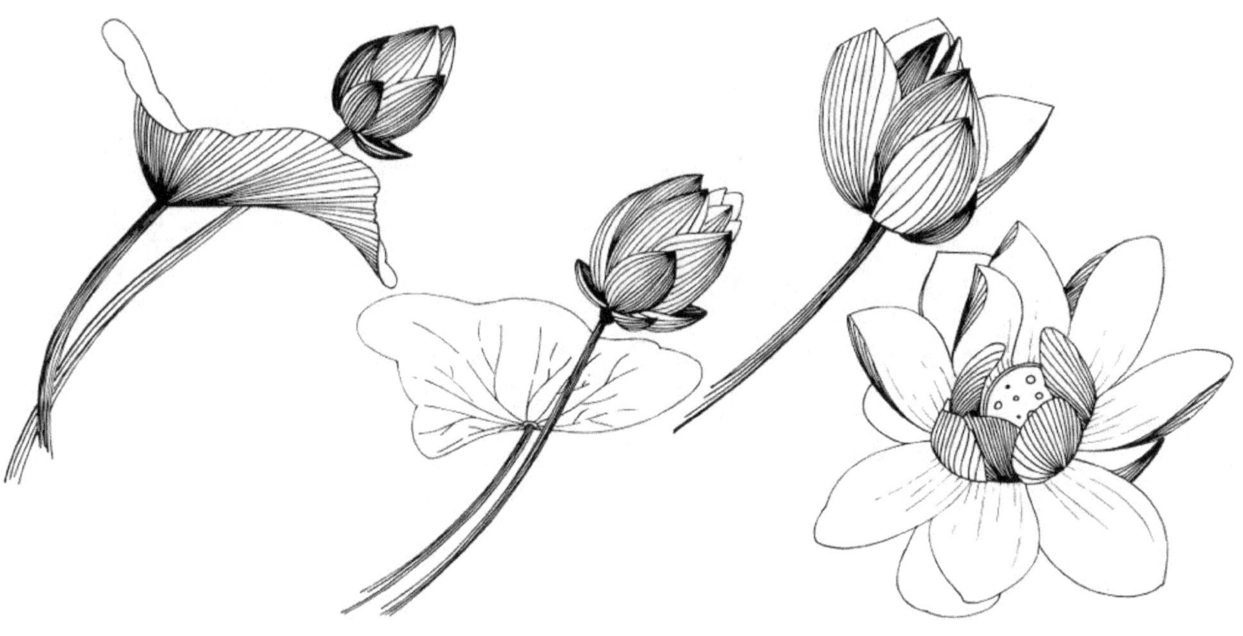

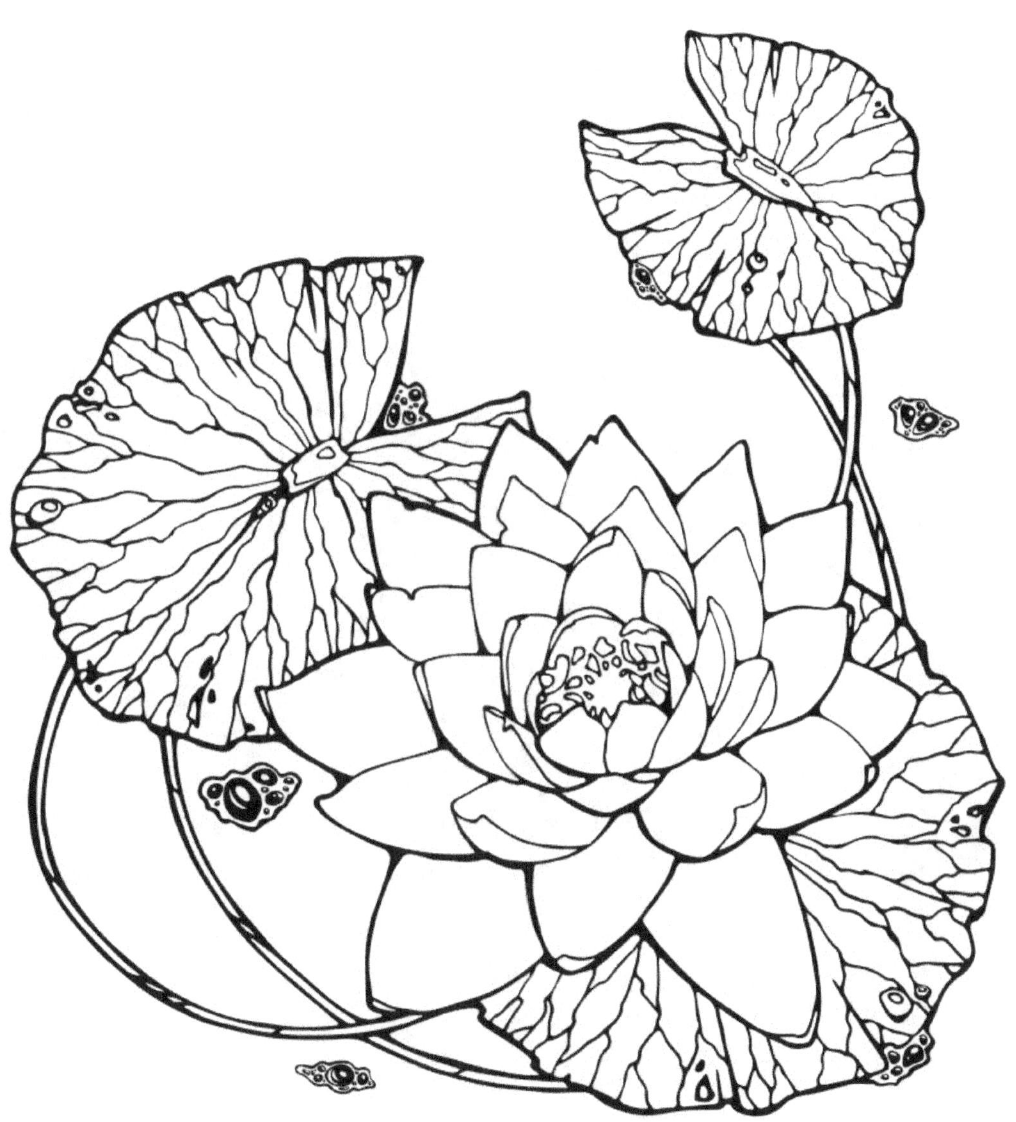

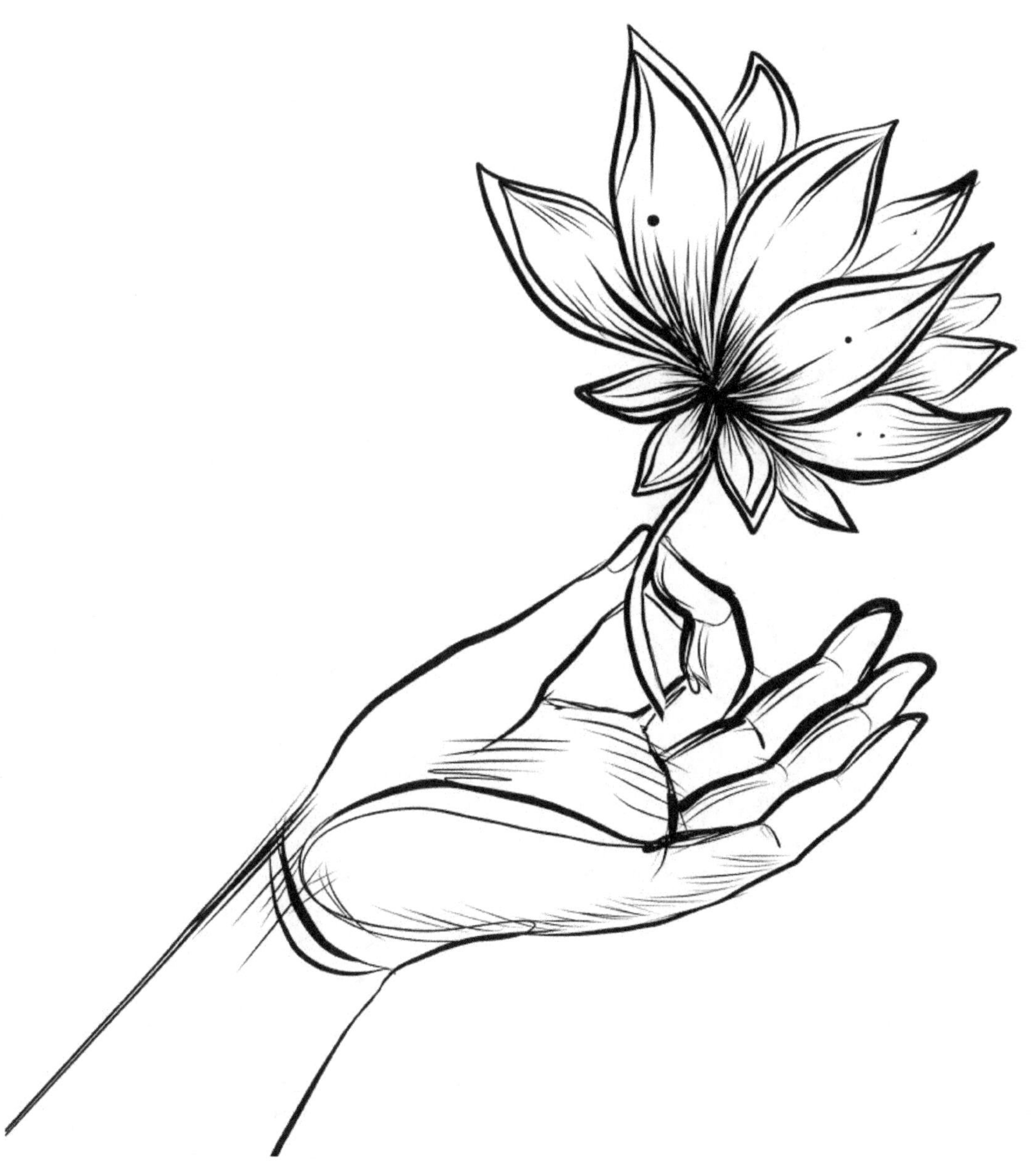

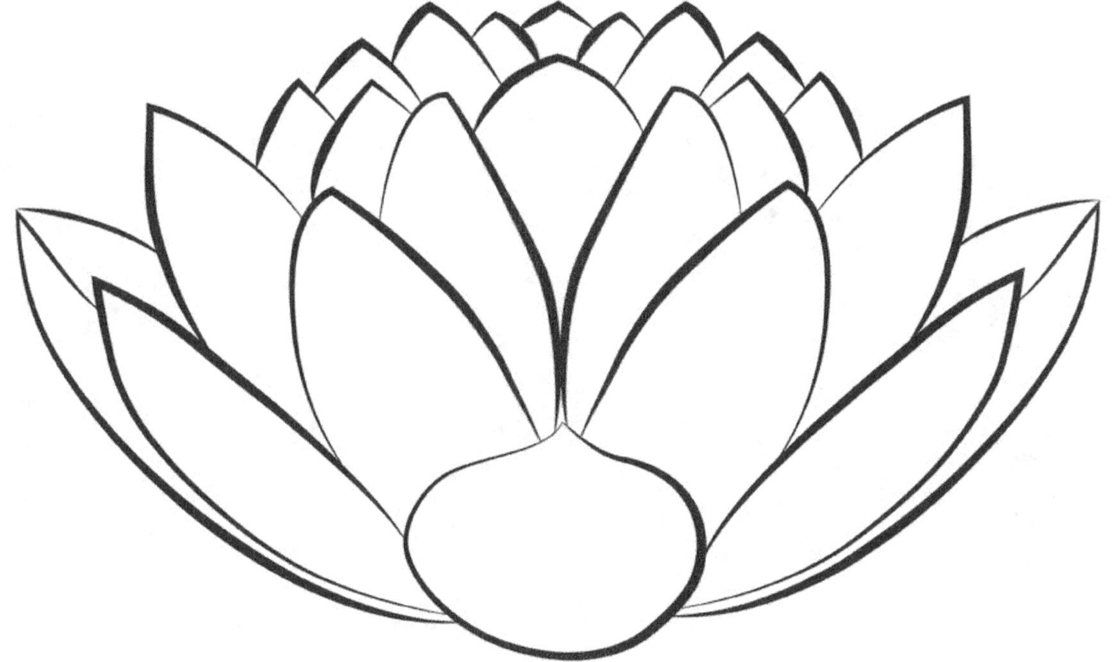

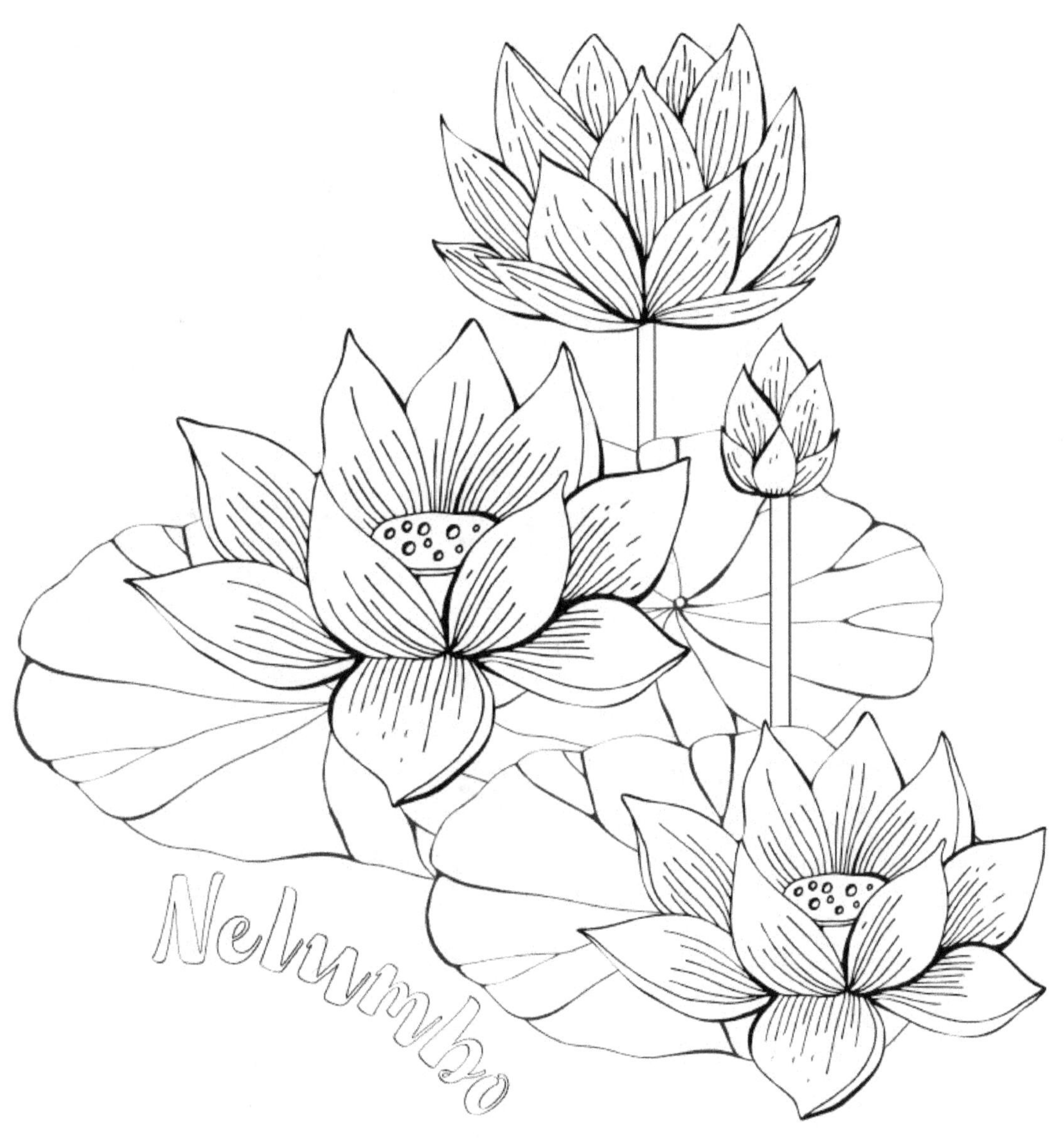

Nelumbo

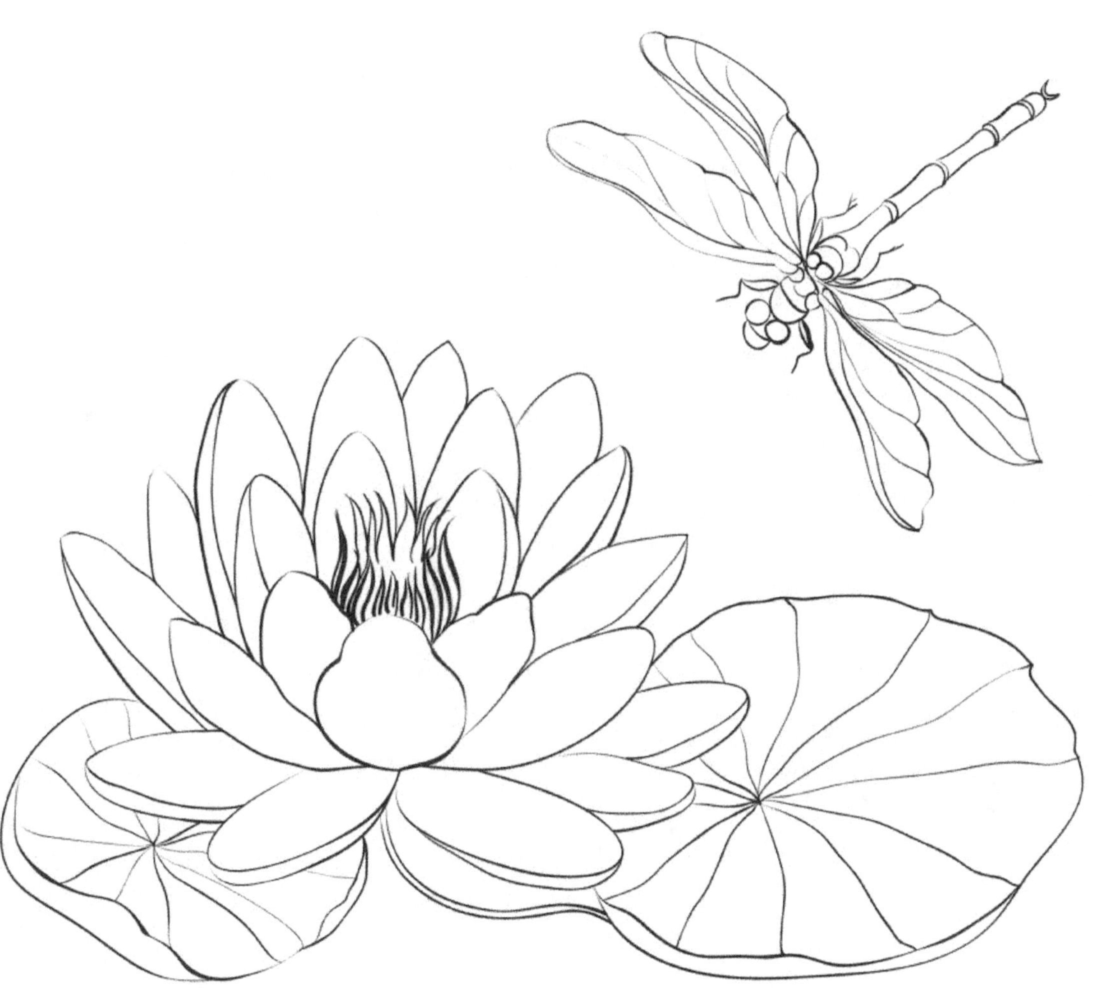

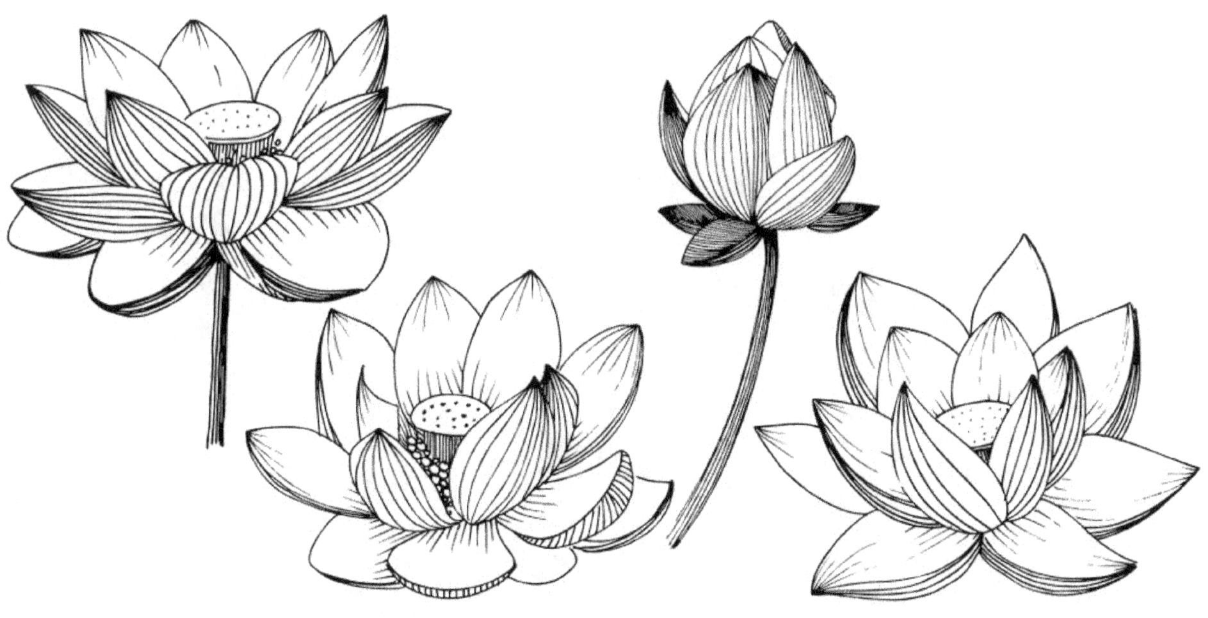

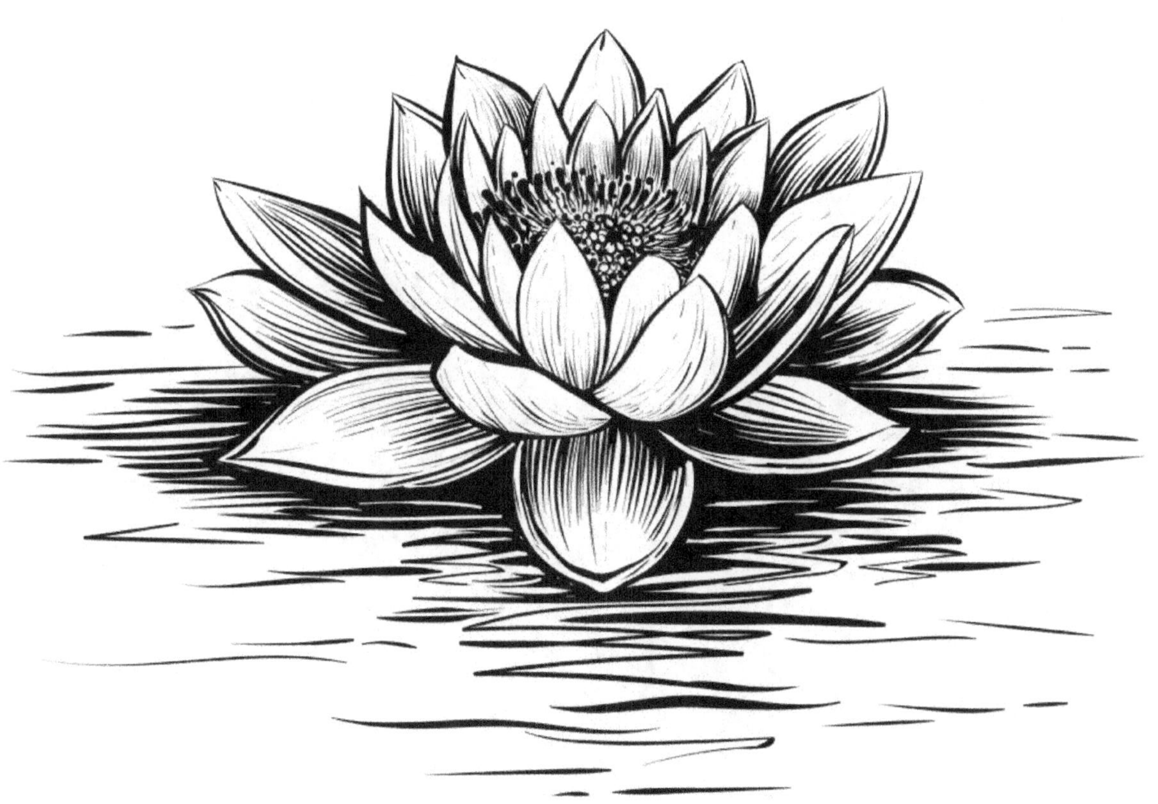

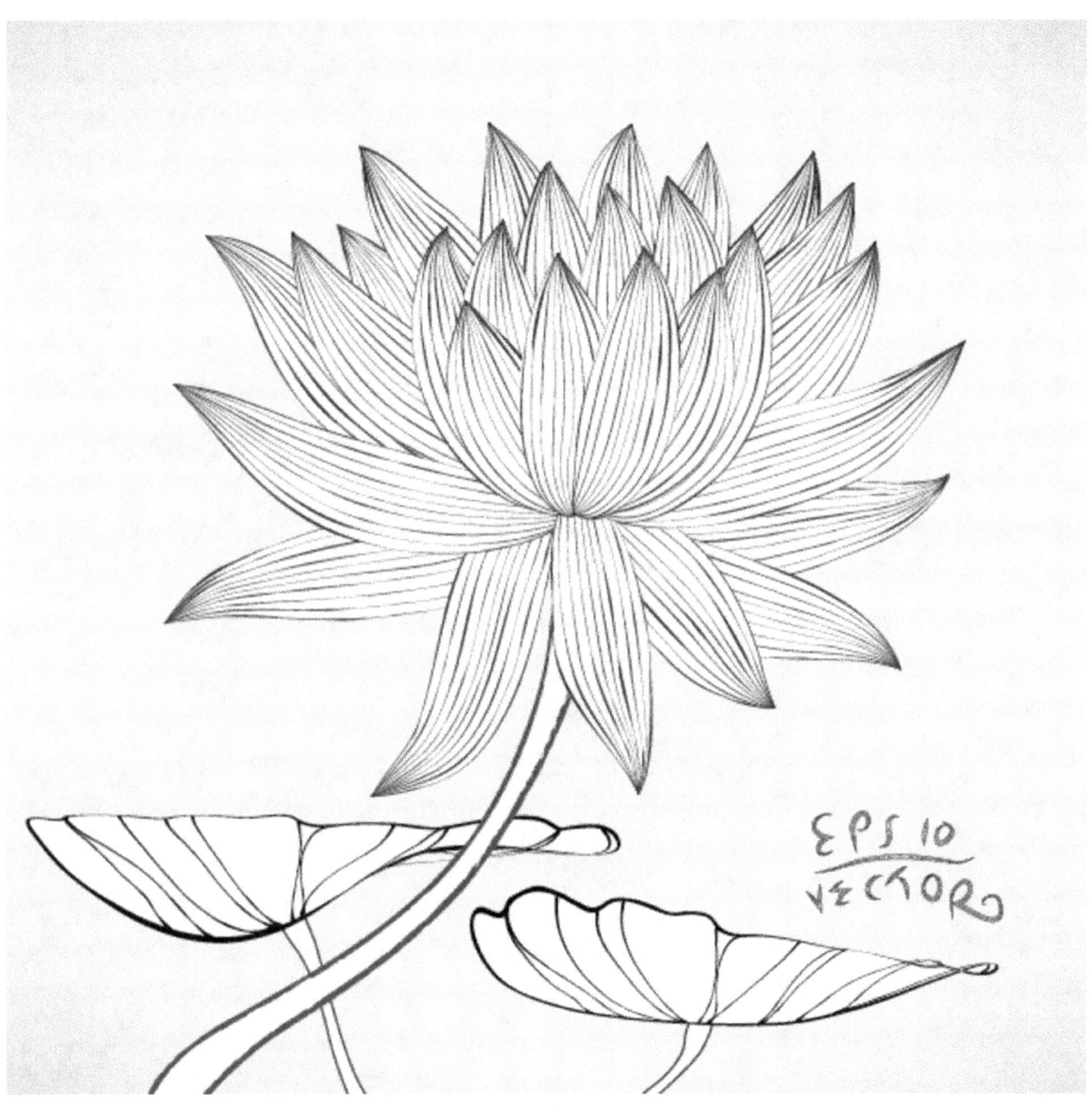

EPS 10
VECTOR

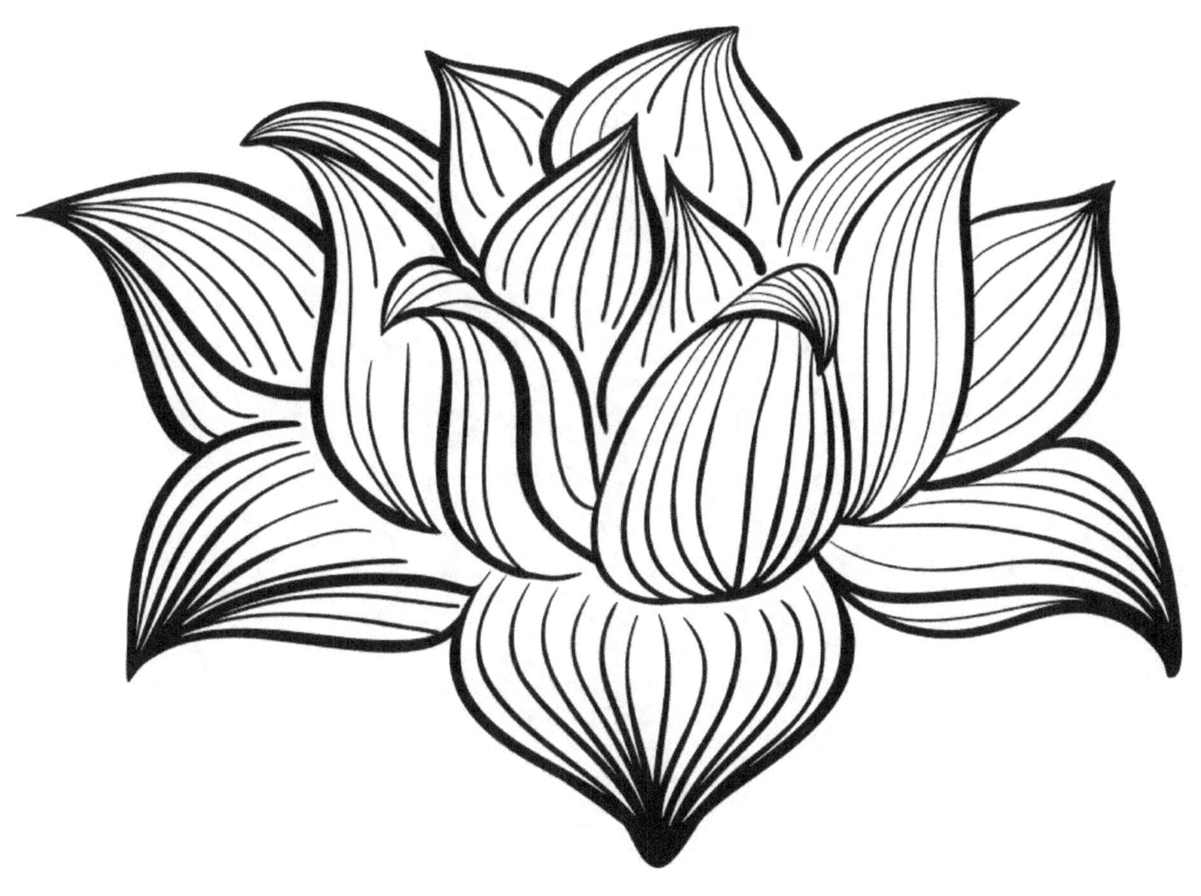

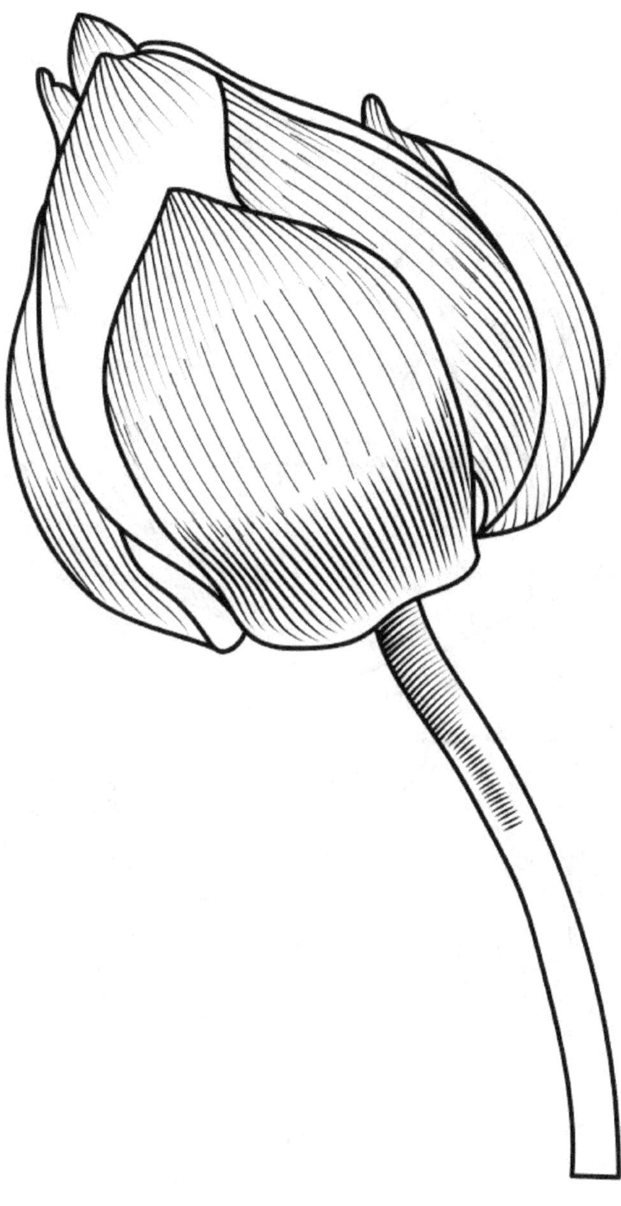

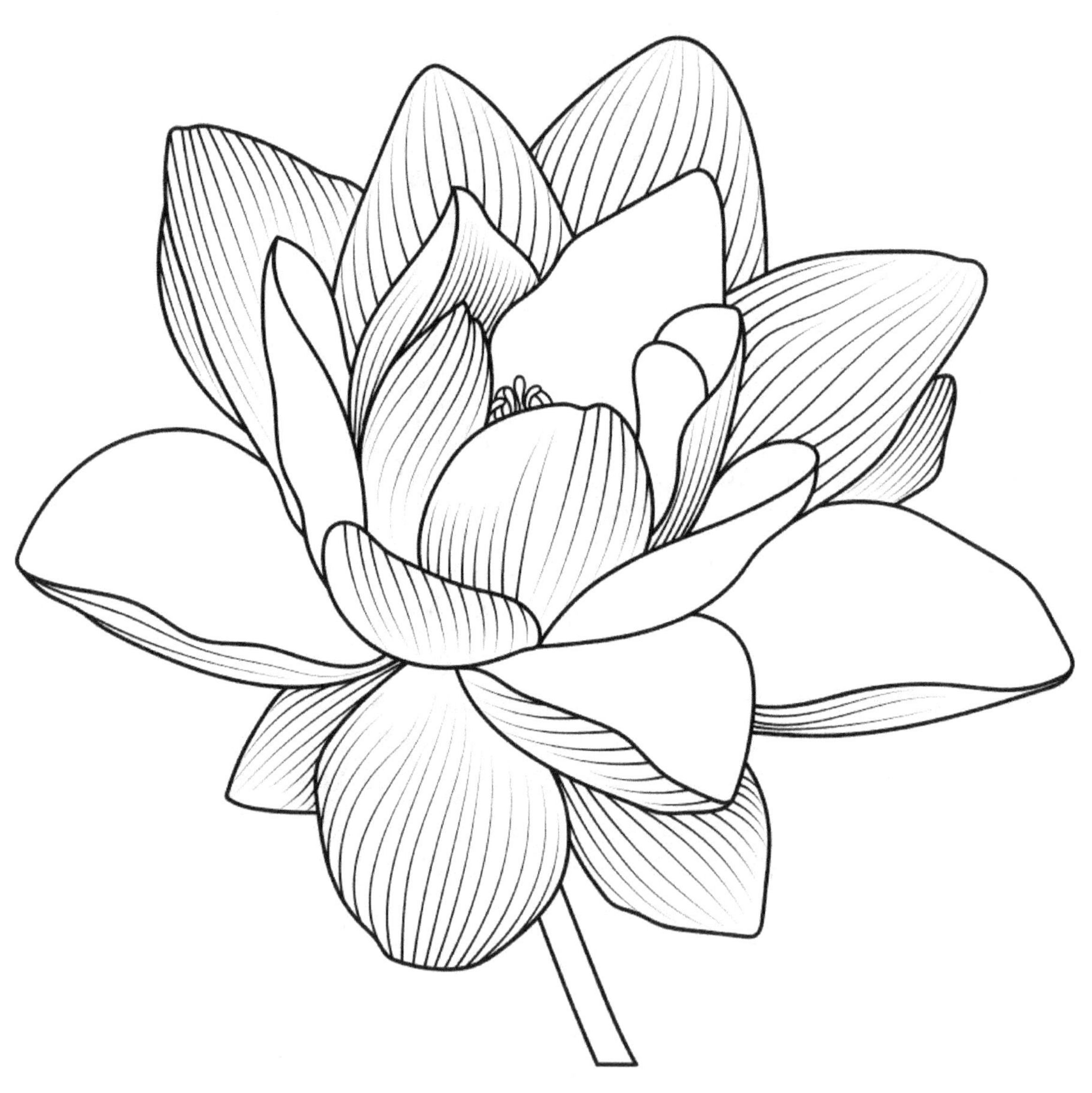

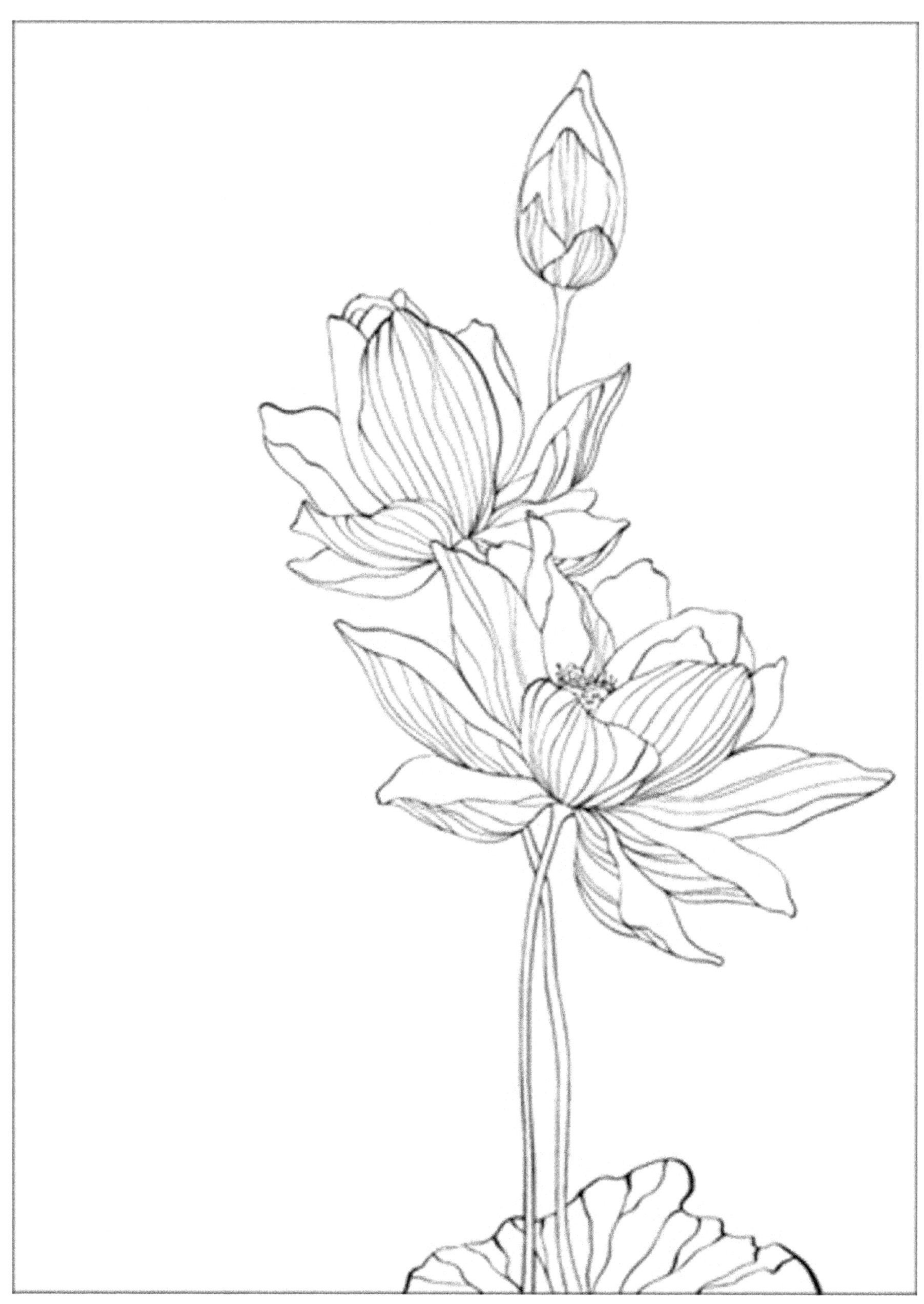